Arbeitsheft: Zum Hören, Sprechen und Schreiben

Sprechen wir Deutsch!

Second Edition

Kathryn A. Corl

Barbara S. Jurasek
Earlham College

Richard T. Jurasek
Earlham College

Holt, Rinehart and Winston, Inc.

New York   Chicago   San Francisco
Philadelphia   Montreal   Toronto
London   Sydney   Tokyo

Credits

132, Reprinted by permission from *Allensbacher Jahrbuch der Demoskopie,* Vol. VII. Verlag für Demoskopie: Allensbach, 1981. **137, 138,** Reprinted by permission of Deutscher Sportbund. **176, 228,** Reprinted by permission of Globus-Kartendienst. **181,** Reprinted by permission of Elefanten Press Verlag.

ISBN 0-03-014103-6

Copyright © 1989, 1985 by Holt, Rinehart and Winston, Inc.

All rights reserved. No part of this publication may be reproduced or transmitted in any form or by any means, electronic or mechanical, including photocopy, recording, or any information storage and retrieval system, without permission in writing from the publisher.

Although for mechanical reasons all pages of this publication are perforated, only those pages imprinted with an HRW copyright notice are intended for removal.

Requests for permission to make copies of any part of the work should be mailed to:
Copyrights and Permissions Department
Holt, Rinehart and Winston, Inc.
Orlando, FL 32887

Printed in the United States of America

9 0 1 2   066   9 8 7 6 5 4 3 2 1

Holt, Rinehart and Winston, Inc.
The Dryden Press
Saunders College Publishing

Preface

The *Arbeitsheft* is designed to accompany the textbook *Sprechen wir Deutsch!* The aim of the workbook is to provide an opportunity for additional practice of oral, listening, and writing skills.

Each chapter of the workbook is divided into Part One, a listening/speaking section, and Part Two, a writing section. Each chapter of *Sprechen wir Deutsch!* has a two-part companion tape of 30 minutes or less per part. The listening/speaking section of each chapter in the *Arbeitsheft* contains the student materials to accompany the tape program. Exercises in the writing section correspond to the grammar presentations within each chapter of *Sprechen wir Deutsch!* and conclude with a *Synthese* section. Activities in the *Synthese* section provide integrated practice of the concepts treated in the chapter as a whole.

The listening/speaking program for each chapter includes the following elements:

- Oral reading by native speakers of German of the *. . . und Funktion* mini-dialogue that corresponds to each **Baustein** grammar topic in the textbook.
- **Aussprache** sections for Chapters 1–7, printed in both the textbook and the lab manual. These sections provide practice in pronouncing individual sounds, words, and complete sentences, using familiar vocabulary.
- **Und Sie?:** a separate listening activity, designed to reinforce new vocabulary introduced in that section of the textbook.
- Listening and speaking activities for each grammar topic in the chapter. These are sequenced from the simple to the more complex, and make possible further practice of chapter grammar and vocabulary. Some activities relating to the grammar sections of the student text are taken directly from or are partially based on the **Im Kontext** sections of the textbook; these are marked with an asterisk. Others complement material appearing in the text. The context of all activities is such that structures can be practiced in real-life situations.
- **Synthese;** end-of-chapter comprehension and production activities. These include a listening passage related to the chapter theme and integrating chapter grammar and vocabulary, followed by a comprehension activity. Also included are personalized questions for oral or written response. Directions and model sentences for each activity are given in the lab manual as well as on tape. For oral exercises, a number is given for each item; for written exercises, blanks for writing are provided.

The writing section provides a series of activities for each grammar topic presented in *Sprechen wir Deutsch!* The activities range from structured exercises to freer communication activities that encourage production of larger segments of written German. The exercises make possible supplementary written practice of the new language structure; the freer activities encourage students to use the new structure in personalized situations. Again, all exercises and activities are set in real-life contexts relating to the chapter themes. Thus student attention is directed toward the meaning and function of language, as well as toward the manipulation of lexical and grammar forms.

The *Arbeitsheft* can be used in a variety of ways, depending on instructional goals and on individual and group needs. The workbook can be assigned on a daily or weekly basis or it can be used for chapter review. Selected workbook activities can also be assigned individually to students who require supplementary work with a particular topic.

K.A.C.

B.S.J.

R.T.J.

Contents

KAPITEL 1 WAS ICH GERN MACHE

PART ONE

I. UND SIE?

Und Sie? Listen to what some students say about some of their activities. Put a check mark under the category that tells what they are talking about. You will hear each statement twice.

BEISPIEL   Ich finde Spanisch and Englisch besonders leicht.

	SPORTS	SCHOOL SUBJECTS	MUSIC
Beispiel	_____	✓ _____	_____
1.	_____	_____	_____
2.	_____	_____	_____
3.	_____	_____	_____
4.	_____	_____	_____
5.	_____	_____	_____
6.	_____	_____	_____
7.	_____	_____	_____
8.	_____	_____	_____

Copyright © 1989 by Holt, Rinehart and Winston, Inc. All rights reserved.

II. AUSSPRACHE

Tenseness, the amount of muscular energy given to the pronunciation of vowel sounds, is an important factor in learning to pronounce the German vowels. Generally, German vowels are pronounced with more energy than English vowels, and they are not glided or diphthongized as are most English vowels.

A. Listen and then repeat these words. Note that in stressed syllables German tense vowels are distinctly longer than their lax counterparts.

tense /i/	spielen die Sie Sabine Biologie wie Musik ihr nie Chemie
lax /ɪ/	Kind Bleistift Bild Professorin Studentin Studentinnen ist ich bitte nicht interessant finden wichtig zwanzig
tense /y/	Tür Bücher Stühle Physik
lax /ʏ/	fünf fünfzehn
tense /u/	du gut Buch Stuhl Kugelschreiber Fußball Student Musik
lax /ʊ/	null minus und Nummer unwichtig
tense /e/	zehn er der sehr geht Wiedersehen
tense /ɛ:/	Käse *(cheese)* Universität *(university)*
lax /ɛ/	gern es Herr Tennis schlecht selten lernen Fenster Wände Männer
tense /ɸ/	Französisch hören
lax /œ/	zwölf
tense /o/	Professor so Oper
lax /ɔ/	besonders Rockmusik oft Volleyball Golf Computerspiele
tense /ɑ:/	na ja Tag Fragen aber gar Tafel
lax /ɑ/	acht das was Volleyball Schach machen Mann danke Land
unstressed /ə/	reise gehe besonders Karten bitte aber lieber

B. Three German vowel sounds have a distinct glide. Pronounce the following words.

/ae/	heißen eins Bleistift reisen leicht Bayern *(Bavaria)*
/ao/	auf Frau auch Umlaut
/ɔɸ/	Fräulein Leute Deutsch Europa

C. Repeat the following sentences, paying special attention to the vowel sounds.

Copyright © 1989 by Holt, Rinehart and Winston, Inc. All rights reserved. **2**

1. Die zwölf Professoren hören oft Oper und Rockmusik.
2. Sabine findet Biologie und Chemie wichtig, aber nicht interessant.
3. Bitte, wie heißen Sie?
4. Frau Mayer und Fräulein Müller lernen Französisch und Deutsch.

III. BAUSTEIN 1.1: VERB CONJUGATIONS AND SUBJECT PRONOUNS

A. . . . und Funktion *(Das macht doch Spaß.)*

B. Was machen Sie gern? A group of people are talking. Tell whether the speaker is talking about one person or more than one. Mark the appropriate column.

BEISPIEL   Ich lerne gern Mathematik.

	ONE	MORE THAN ONE
Beispiel	✓	
1.		
2.		
3.		
4.		
5.		

C. Sie oder du? Several people are getting acquainted at a party. Listen to what they say, and decide whether the speakers are using the formal form or the informal form. Mark the appropriate column.

BEISPIEL   Ich tanze gern. Und Sie?
           Ja, ich auch.

	FORMAL	INFORMAL
Beispiel	✓	
1.		
2.		

Polizisten duzen kostet 300 Mark

„Du blöde Sau" sagte ein Mann aus Ravensburg zum Grenzpolizisten – und wurde vom Amtsgericht Lindau zu 2 500 Mark Strafe verurteilt. Seinen Freund kostete das vertrauliche „Du" (ohne Zusatz) 300 Mark. Der Richter: „Beleidigung".

Copyright © 1989 by Holt, Rinehart and Winston, Inc. All rights reserved.

3. _____ _____

4. _____ _____

5. _____ _____

D. Was lernen sie? Students in the library at the **Universität Wien** (University of Vienna) are discussing what subjects they are studying tonight. What do they say?

BEISPIEL   Paul: Physik
Ich lerne Physik.

Maria und Bernd: Mathematik
Wir lernen Mathematik.

1   2   3   4   5

IV.   BAUSTEIN 1.2: NEGATION WITH <u>NICHT</u>

A. . . . und Funktion *(Am Telefon.)*

B. Machen sie das? A group of students are talking about their activities. For each activity, decide whether it is something that the speaker or another person does or does not do. If the person does the activity, underline **ja.** If the person doesn't do the activity, underline **nein.**

BEISPIEL   Ich arbeite nie.

Beispiel ja   <u>nein</u>

1. ja   nein   2. ja   nein
3. ja   nein   4. ja   nein
5. ja   nein   6. ja   nein

C. Welches Bild? (Which picture?) For each sentence you hear, circle the letter of the picture that best suggests its meaning.

Copyright © 1989 by Holt, Rinehart and Winston, Inc. All rights reserved.   **4**

BEISPIEL   Er schwimmt nicht sehr gut.

 A

B

1.   A

B

2.   A

B

Copyright © 1989 by Holt, Rinehart and Winston, Inc. All rights reserved.   **5**

3. **A**    **B**

4. **A**    **B**

*D. Klagen, Klagen. (Complaints, complaints.) Manfred is complaining about his roommate Heinrich, who doesn't seem to do anything right. What does Manfred say?

BEISPIEL   Ich tanze gut . . .

      . . . aber er tanzt nicht gut.

1   2   3   4   5   6

Copyright © 1989 by Holt, Rinehart and Winston, Inc. All rights reserved.

V. BAUSTEIN 1.3: INTERROGATIVES

A. . . . und Funktion *(Ein Survey.)*

B. Fragen? Listen to what the following people say, and decide whether you hear a question each time. Put a check mark under the column marked "question" if the sentence you hear is a question, and a check mark under the column marked "statement" if it isn't.

BEISPIEL   Tanzt er gut?

	STATEMENT	**QUESTION**
Beispiel	_____	✓_____
1.	_____	_____
2.	_____	_____
3.	_____	_____
4.	_____	_____
5.	_____	_____
6.	_____	_____
7.	_____	_____
8.	_____	_____

C. Fragen, Fragen. Gerhard is going to introduce Renate to his friend Erik. She wants to know all about him before she meets him. What does she ask? Use the cues as a guide.

BEISPIEL   spielen/gut/Tennis?
           Spielt er gut Tennis?

1   2   3   4   5

Copyright © 1989 by Holt, Rinehart and Winston, Inc. All rights reserved.

VI. BAUSTEIN 1.4: VERBS WITH STEM-VOWEL CHANGES

A. . . . und Funktion *(Familienstreit.)*

B. In der Mensa (In the cafeteria). A group of students are talking in the **Mensa** at the **Universität Heidelberg.** For each set of sentences you hear, indicate whether the speaker is talking to one or more than one person.

BEISPIEL   Ich esse Joghurt und Obst. Was eßt ihr?

	ONE	MORE THAN ONE
Beispiel	_____	__✓__
1.	_____	_____
2.	_____	_____
3.	_____	_____
4.	_____	_____
5.	_____	_____
6.	_____	_____

C. Ich lese gern . . .   Some friends are talking about what they like to read. What do they say? Use the cues.

BEISPIEL   ich/Zeitungen
          Ich lese gern Zeitungen.

1   2   3   4   5

VII. SYNTHESE

A. Ein Kassetten-Freund.   Roberta has joined an international cassette exchange club, and has just received her first tape from the Bundesrepublik. Listen to the passage on the tape. Then stop the tape

Copyright © 1989 by Holt, Rinehart and Winston, Inc. All rights reserved.

and decide whether or not Roberta has understood it by marking her statements **richtig** (true) or **falsch** (false). You will hear the passage twice.

1. Gerd is from West Berlin.   **richtig falsch**
2. He is majoring in physics at the university in West Berlin.
   richtig falsch
3. He doesn't like to do math because it is very difficult.   **richtig falsch**
4. His hobby is learning languages.   **richtig falsch**
5. He speaks Italian very well.   **richtig falsch**
6. He is going to Spain.   **richtig falsch**
7. The mountains are one of his favorite travel spots.   **richtig falsch**

B. Und Sie?   An Austrian exchange student wants to know about your interests. Answer the questions in the pauses provided. Each question will be asked twice.

1   2   3   4   5   6   7   8

Copyright © 1989 by Holt, Rinehart and Winston, Inc. All rights reserved.

PART TWO

I. BAUSTEIN 1.1: VERB CONJUGATIONS AND SUBJECT PRONOUNS

A. Im Hotel.   The following comments were overheard in a hotel lobby at a vacation resort. Recreate the tourists' comments. Write the correct form of the verb that best completes the meaning of the sentence.

1. Man _____ Schach und Domino im Hotel.   (spielen/

    heißen)

2. Und Sie, Frau Anker, _____ Sie Jazzmusik gern?

    (reisen/hören)

3. Peter? Er _____ oft.   (reisen/heißen)

4. Elfriede und Thomas, _____ ihr gern?   (verstehen/

    schwimmen)

5. Wir _____ Tischtennis nie langweilig.   (finden/spielen)

B. Was ich gern mache.   Combine words from the balloon with the verbs below to create sentences that express individually or collectively your likes, dislikes, and activities.

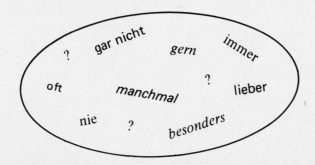

Copyright © 1989 by Holt, Rinehart and Winston, Inc. All rights reserved.   **11**

BEISPIEL finden

Ich finde Deutsch besonders leicht.
Wir finden Computerspiele besonders interessant.

1. rauchen _____

2. arbeiten _____

3. reisen _____

4. lernen _____

5. spielen _____

II. BAUSTEIN 1.2: NEGATION WITH <u>NICHT</u>

A. Falsch! Monika and a group of friends disagree with comments made about them by others. Recreate their responses by putting the following sentences in the negative.

BEISPIEL Volker hört gern klassische Musik.
Falsch! Er hört nicht gern klassische Musik.

1. Gerda raucht oft.

   _____

2. Herr und Frau Fichte lernen gern Philosophie.

   _____

3. Du hörst gern Oper.

   _____

4. Ich tanze immer.

   _____

5. Ursula arbeitet.

   _____

Copyright © 1989 by Holt, Rinehart and Winston, Inc. All rights reserved.

6. Fritz versteht das.

_____

B. Und Sie? Make a list of things you dislike or don't do often.

BEISPIEL   Ich singe nicht gern.

1. _____

2. _____

3. _____

4. _____

5. _____

III. BAUSTEIN 1.3: INTERROGATIVES

A. Fragen, Fragen.   Franz is talking with Susanne and wants to find out about her and her roommate Julia. What questions would he ask to obtain the following information?

BEISPIEL   If she plays ping-pong
           Spielst du Tischtennis?

1. If Susanne is learning French

_____

2. If they travel often

_____

3. If Julia sometimes goes hiking

_____

4. How often Julia listens to music

_____

5. What they like to do

_____

Copyright © 1989 by Holt, Rinehart and Winston, Inc. All rights reserved.

6. Who plays volleyball

_____

B. Konversation.   Write questions that Herta might have asked
Albert about himself or his friends Stefan and Max.

BEISPIEL   Albert: Ja, wir lernen Englisch gern.
            Herta: Lernt ihr Englisch gern?
              or: **Ihr lernt Englisch gern, nicht wahr?**

1. Herta: _____
   Albert: Nein, ich finde Physik gar nicht interessant.

2. Herta: _____
   Albert: Wir spielen immer Karten.

3. Herta: _____
   Albert: Nein, Stefan und Max finden das nicht besonders schwer.

4. Herta: _____
   Albert: Nein, er hört immer Rockmusik.

5. Herta: _____
   Albert: Na ja, ich arbeite manchmal.

IV.   BAUSTEIN 1.4: VERBS WITH STEM-VOWEL CHANGES

A. Aber du . . . !   Rolf is one of those people who always does
things better. Write the correct form of the verb.

1. Ich _____ gern Obst, aber du _____ lieber

   Schokolade! (essen)

2. Ich _____ immer langsam, aber du _____ oft

   sehr schnell! (fahren)

3. Ich _____ Englisch gut, aber du _____

   Englisch schlecht! (sprechen)

Copyright © 1989 by Holt, Rinehart and Winston, Inc. All rights reserved.

4. Ich _____ gern Literatur, aber du _____ lieber

Comic-Hefte! (lesen)

B. Jeder ist anders.   (Everybody's different.) Use the following verbs to write sentences comparing your preferences or actions to those of others in the classroom.

BEISPIEL   **Die Professorin spricht Deutsch schnell, aber ich spreche langsam.**

1. spielen _____

2. lesen _____

3. hören _____

4. fahren _____

V. SYNTHESE

A. Mini-Dialog.   Using the vocabulary you have learned so far, complete the following conversation between Jens and Gerda.

Jens: Ich sehe Filme gern. Und du?

Gerda: _____

Jens: _____

Gerda: _____

B. Was sie machen, und was sie denken.   Imagine that you meet the four people from the **Synthese** reading in Chapter 1. Create a question that you might ask each one in order to find out what they do and think.

Copyright © 1989 by Holt, Rinehart and Winston, Inc. All rights reserved.

BEISPIEL   **Cécile, finden Sie Politik interessant?**
Gabriele, studieren Sie gern Architektur?

1. Cécile: _____

   _____

2. Gabriele: _____

   _____

3. Manfred: _____

   _____

4. Ewald: _____

   _____

Copyright © 1989 by Holt, Rinehart and Winston, Inc. All rights reserved.

KAPITEL **2 WIE ICH BIN UND WAS ICH HABE**

PART ONE

I. UND SIE?

Positiv oder negativ? A multinational corporation is reviewing candidates for an office position. Listen to what each person says about the candidates, and put a check mark under the column marked **positiv** or **negativ** for each characteristic you hear.

BEISPIEL   Herr Schwarz ist intelligent, aber unrealistisch.

		POSITIV	NEGATIV
Beispiel	a.	✓	
	b.		✓
1. Frau Müller:	a.		
	b.		
2. Herr Neumann:	a.		
	b.		
3. Fräulein Liebermann:	a.		
	b.		

Copyright © 1989 by Holt, Rinehart and Winston, Inc. All rights reserved.

4. Frau Obermayer: a. _____   _____

                       b. _____   _____

5. Herr Lenz: .a. _____   _____

                       b. _____   _____

II.   AUSSPRACHE

The rounded front vowels, or **umlauts,** do not exist in English. The vowel pairs /y/ and /Y/ are pronounced as the vowels /i/ and /I/, as in **Sie** and **bitte,** except that the lips are rounded and protruded to the front. The vowels /ϕ/ and /œ/ are pronounced as the vowels /e/ as in **geht** and /ɛ/ as in **es** with lip rounding.

A.   Listen and then repeat the following words. Note the contrasted vowel sounds.

/ɪ/ vs. /y/		/ɪ/ vs. /Y/		/e/ vs. /ϕ/		/ɛ/ vs. /œ/	
Biene	Bühne	sticke	Stücke	lese	löse	kennen	können
Kien	kühn	Lifte	Lüfte	sehne	Söhne	Stecke	Stöcke

B.   Listen to the tape, then repeat the following words.

/y/   für Zürich über natürlich Bücher Physik
/Y/   Düsseldorf fünf fünfzehn
/ϕ/   schön höflich Französisch hören Österreich blöd
/œ/   zwölf Köln

C.   Repeat the following sentences, paying close attention to the rounded front vowel sounds.

1.   Natürlich sind die Bücher für Sie.
2.   Wir hören viel über Zürich und Düsseldorf, aber wenig über Köln.
3.   Günter und Jörg finden Physik blöd.

III.   BAUSTEIN 2.1: THE VERBS SEIN AND HABEN

A.   . . . und Funktion (Besuch.)

B. Horoskop.   While on a bus tour of Austria, a group of American students and their host families are reading horoscopes. For each

Copyright © 1989 by Holt, Rinehart and Winston, Inc. All rights reserved.

sentence you hear, decide whether the comments made are about one or more than one person. Indicate your answer by placing a check mark under the appropriate column. You will hear each sentence twice.

BEISPIEL   Ihr seid fleißig, aber unrealistisch.

	ONE	**MORE THAN ONE**
Beispiel	_____	____✓____
1.	_____	_____
2.	_____	_____
3.	_____	_____
4.	_____	_____
5.	_____	_____
6.	_____	_____

*C. Reisebemerkungen   (Travel notes). Brigitte is on a tour and makes comments about the things she experiences. Tell what she says.

BEISPIEL   Museum/interessant
          Das Museum ist interessant.

1   2   3   4   5   6

*D. Wer bringt was?   Several students are organizing a sale to raise money for a trip. They are talking about who has what items to sell. What do they say?

BEISPIEL   Bernd/Platten
          Bernd hat Platten.

1   2   3   4   5   6

Copyright © 1989 by Holt, Rinehart and Winston, Inc. All rights reserved.   **19**

IV. BAUSTEIN 2.2: CASE: NOMINATIVE AND ACCUSATIVE

A. ... und Funktion *(Entscheidungen.)*

B. Wir ziehen um! (Moving day!) Jens and Sigrid are helping Astrid move. Listen to the following excerpts from their conversation, and decide whether the pronouns that refer to the items mentioned are in the nominative or the accusative case in each sentence. You will hear each excerpt twice.

BEISPIEL   Der Tisch? Wir haben ihn!

	NOMINATIVE	**ACCUSATIVE**
Beispiel	_____	____✓____
1.	_____	_____
2.	_____	_____
3.	_____	_____
4.	_____	_____
5.	_____	_____
6.	_____	_____

*C. Was sagen sie?   Max is asking Brigitte about her friends' opinions on a number of things. Give Brigitte's answers.

BEISPIEL   Wie findet Hans die Zeitung? (langweilig)
        Er findet sie langweilig.

1   2   3   4   5   6

Copyright © 1989 by Holt, Rinehart and Winston, Inc. All rights reserved.   **20**

V. BAUSTEIN 2.3: PREPOSITIONS WITH THE ACCUSATIVE

A. . . . und Funktion *(Andere Pläne.)*

B. Schlechte Verbindungen. (Bad connections.) Roberta has just returned from a trip and is trying to talk with her friends on the phone, but the connection is bad. Underline the phrase that best completes each sentence.

BEISPIEL   Bringst du Süßigkeiten . . .
   a. für die Kinder   b. durch die Tür   c. ohne die Zeitung

1. a. gegen dich?   b. für mich?   c. um sie?
2. a. durchs Land   b. ums Auto   c. gegen die Schweiz
3. a. ohne Hunde   b. für Haustiere   c. gegen Katzen
4. a. gegen mich   b. durch ihn   c. ohne dich

*C. Ich sehe es anders.   (I see it differently.) In nearly every conversation Rainer feels compelled to add his own perspective to change whatever has been said. Use the cues to tell what Rainer says.

BEISPIEL   Die Wohnung ist sauber ohne die Katze.   (Hund)
   Moment mal! Die Wohnung ist sauber ohne den Hund.

1   2   3   4   5   6

VI. BAUSTEIN 2.4: <u>EIN</u>-WORDS: POSSESSIVE ADJECTIVES AND <u>KEIN</u>

A. . . . und Funktion *(Dieses Mal nicht!)*

B. Familie Penz.   The housekeeper is helping Professor Penz's family pack for a month's vacation in Mexico. Listen to what she says, and determine whether each statement or question is directed at Professor Penz, his daughter Julia, or the twins, Georg and Trude. You will hear each statement twice.

Copyright © 1989 by Holt, Rinehart and Winston, Inc. All rights reserved.   **21**

BEISPIEL   Eure Comic-Hefte sind nicht wichtig.

	JULIA	**PROFESSOR PENZ**	**GEORG UND TRUDE**
Beispiel	_____	_____	✓ _____
1.	_____	_____	_____
2.	_____	_____	_____
3.	_____	_____	_____
4.	_____	_____	_____
5.	_____	_____	_____
6.	_____	_____	_____
7.	_____	_____	_____

C. Was kaufen wir?   The Herzls are discussing gifts to buy for
various family members. Listen to what they say, and for each person
mentioned, cross out the pictures of the items the Herzls think the
person already has or does not need. Circle the items the Herzls think
are good gift suggestions. You will hear each exchange twice.

BEISPIEL   Franz? O, er hat viele Kassetten und Platten.
           **Ja, aber er hat keinen Kassettenrecorder. Wir kaufen einen
           Kassettenrecorder.**

Franz:

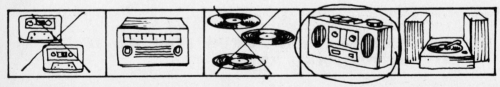

1. Dieter:

Copyright © 1989 by Holt, Rinehart and Winston, Inc. All rights reserved.   **22**

2. Jürgen und Astrid:

3. Professor Klahr:

4. Anneliese:

D. Haben sie alles? (Do they have everything?) Stefan's father is watching Dora and Stefan pack their car for their return to the university after summer vacation. He wonders whether they have remembered to take everything. What does he ask himself?

BEISPIEL   Dora: die Gitarre
            Hat sie ihre Gitarre?

1   2   3   4   5   6

VII. SYNTHESE

A. Liebe Susanne . . .   Susanne Hagen has just received an answer to her letter from Fred Miller. In it, Fred answers the questions she had asked and describes the members of his family. Listen as she reads the letter to a friend; then stop the tape and write the answers to the questions in English. The letter will be read twice.

1.   What adjectives describe Fred's brother Stan?

_____

Copyright © 1989 by Holt, Rinehart and Winston, Inc. All rights reserved.

2. How old is Fred's sister Kathy? What adjectives describe her?

   _____

3. What do we know about Fred's parents?

   _____

4. How is life for Fred at the university?

   _____

5. What does Fred consider to be a problem?

   _____

6. What is Fred's major?

   _____

B. Ein Interview.   Imagine that in an interview you are asked to talk about your family and yourself. You may wish to include the following points: (1) How many brothers and sisters you have; (2) What adjectives would describe them; (3) What your parents are like; (4) Other relatives and their characteristics; (5) How old you are and what adjectives describe you. You may formulate your thoughts in the form of brief notes in German. Begin speaking when you hear the tone.

_____

_____

_____

_____

_____

_____

_____

Copyright © 1989 by Holt, Rinehart and Winston, Inc. All rights reserved.

PART TWO

I. BAUSTEIN 2.1: THE VERBS SEIN AND HABEN

A. Persönlichkeitstest.   A group of students have taken a person-ality test. Beate is tabulating the results and is writing to her absent friends Jörg and Wilhelmine. Complete the following excerpts from the letter with the appropriate forms of the verbs **haben** and **sein.**

1. Der Kontakt mit Menschen _____ sehr wichtig. Ich

    _____ nicht gern allein.

2. Georg _____ die Natur gern; er _____ sehr

    romantisch.

3. Karl und Helga _____ viele Instrumente; Musik und Kunst

    _____ besonders wichtig für sie.

4. Jörg, du _____ nicht zu optimistisch, aber auch nicht zu

    pessimistisch.

5. Ihr _____ nie müde, und ihr _____ viel Energie.

6. Wir _____ ziemlich traditionell und konservativ.

7. Ich _____ praktisch und unkompliziert.

B. Die Reisegruppe.   Professor Hampton has collected information that will help an Austrian agency find housing for her and a student group. Translate the notes she has made.

Copyright © 1989 by Holt, Rinehart and Winston, Inc. All rights reserved.
        25

1. Carole likes music, especially opera.

   _____

2. Irena and David like films and politics.

   _____

3. Kathy likes pets, especially dogs.

   _____

4. We don't like fast-food restaurants!

   _____

5. Amanda and Robin like mountains and nature.

   _____

6. I like books, especially novels.

   _____

C. Meiner Meinung nach. (In my opinion.) Complete each of the following sentences so that they express your personal reactions. Use the appropriate form of **sein** and one or more adjectives.

1. Comic-Hefte _____

2. Ich _____

3. Die Universität _____

4. Das Leben _____

II. BAUSTEIN 2.2: CASE: NOMINATIVE AND ACCUSATIVE

A. Jochens Zimmer. Shown below is Jochen's room. Using the vocabulary you know, make a list of things found in his room.

Copyright © 1989 by Holt, Rinehart and Winston, Inc. All rights reserved.

BEISPIEL   Was ist im Zimmer?   Was hat Jochen?

ein Schreibtisch   **einen Schreibtisch**

	Was ist im Zimmer?	**Was hat Jochen?**
1.	_____	_____
2.	_____	_____
3.	_____	_____
4.	_____	_____
5.	_____	_____
6.	_____	_____
7.	_____	_____
8.	_____	_____

Copyright © 1989 by Holt, Rinehart and Winston, Inc. All rights reserved.

9. _____   _____

10. _____   _____

B. Kaum zu glauben! (Hard to believe!) Johann is feeling argumentative today. Complete the following sentences to tell what he says to some of his friends.

BEISPIEL   Du findest den Computer teuer? Ich finde **ihn** ziemlich billig.

1. Du hast einen Hund? Ich höre und sehe _____ aber nicht!

2. Du liebst das Leben? Ich finde _____ sehr schwer!

3. Du liest den Roman? Ich finde _____ langweilig!

4. Du kaufst die Gitarre? Ich finde _____ zu teuer!

5. Du hast den Film gern? Ich finde _____ schlecht!

6. Du hast Haustiere gern? Ich habe _____ gar nicht gern!

III.   BAUSTEIN 2.3: PREPOSITIONS WITH THE ACCUSATIVE

A. Der erste Tag.   Following are excerpts from various letters Sabine has written after her first day at the university. Write the German equivalents of the words in parentheses.

1. Ich brauche einen Schreibtisch _____

   (for the room).

2. Erich, ich bin unglücklich _____ (without

   you).

3. Ich denke, die Professoren sind _____

   (against me).

4. Ich höre immer Musik _____ (through the

   wall).

Copyright © 1989 by Holt, Rinehart and Winston, Inc. All rights reserved.   **28**

5. Das Leben ist nicht leicht _____ *(without a*

car).

B. Wie sagt man . . . ? Give the German equivalent for the following sentences or phrases.

1. The picture is for the gentleman.

   _____

2. The roses are for the student *(male).*

   _____

3. without a name _____

4. The candy is for me!

   _____

5. against the door _____

6. around the cathedral _____

7. a life without hobbies _____

8. through the window _____

IV. BAUSTEIN 2.4: <u>EIN</u>-WORDS: POSSESSIVE ADJECTIVES AND <u>KEIN</u>

A. Was ich habe. Udo is telling Heinrich the various things they and their friends do and don't possess. For each numbered item below, select a related item from the list and combine them according to the model, so as to reconstruct Udo's sentences.

Zeitungen	Kugelschreiber
Motorrad	Stereoanlage
Wohnung	Computer
Stuhl	Schreibtisch

Copyright © 1989 by Holt, Rinehart and Winston, Inc. All rights reserved.

BEISPIEL   Ich: Bleistift
           Ich habe einen Bleistift, aber keinen Kugelschreiber.

1. Wir: Tisch

    _____

2. Ihr: Magazine

    _____

3. Die Studenten: Taschenrechner

    _____

4. Du: Zimmer

    _____

5. Albert: Fahrrad

    _____

6. Ingeborg: Radio

    _____

B. Im Büro.   (At the office.) The following comments were overheard
on a typical day at the office. Recreate the employees' comments by
filling in the blanks with the appropriate form of the possessive adjectives in parentheses.

1. Herr Weigel, Sie bringen _____ Schreibmaschine, nicht

    wahr? *(your)*

2. Braucht ihr _____ Bleistifte? *(your)*

3. Einen Moment, Ulla. Ich brauche _____ Taschenrechner.

    (your)

4. Christa Wolf? Ich finde _____ Romane sehr gut. *(her)*

Copyright © 1989 by Holt, Rinehart and Winston, Inc. All rights reserved.   **30**

5. Ich kaufe Pflanzen für _____ Zimmer. (our)

6. Fassbinder? Ja, ich habe _____ Filme gern. (his)

7. Na ja, _____ Wohnung ist nett, aber zu klein und zu teuer.

   (my)

C. Und Sie?   Complete the following sentences so that they are true for you or the persons indicated. Use a form of **kein** or a possessive adjective in each sentence.

BEISPIEL   Ich brauche **eine Uhr für mein Zimmer.**

1. Ich brauche _____

2. Ich kaufe _____

3. Ein(e) Student(in) ist nie ohne _____

4. Viele Leute kaufen _____

5. Ich habe _____

6. Meine Freunde haben _____

V. SYNTHESE

A. Robert Dorn.   In the following passage Renate Dorn's brother is writing about himself. Fill in the blanks with the appropriate word in order to make complete and meaningful sentences. In some places there is only one right answer; in others there are several possibilities.

Ich _____ Robert. Ich bin Renates _____.

_____ Schwester und ich _____ in Hamburg, denn

wir _____ auf der Universität. _____ Bruder

Adrian ist zehn Jahre alt und sehr _____. Renate und ich besu-

chen _____ Familie oft.

Ich _____ _____ Berge und _____

Copyright © 1989 by Holt, Rinehart and Winston, Inc. All rights reserved.

gern. Ich _____ gern Briefe. Ich _____ ziemlich oft

_____ . Und ohne _____ Hund bin ich sehr traurig!

_____ Freunde sagen, ich bin _____ und

_____ und habe immer genug Zeit für _____ .

Meine Geschwister sagen, ich bin _____ . Und

_____ Freundin? Sie sagt, ich bin _____ !

B. Using the questions below as a guide, write a paragraph describing the typical American college student to a Swiss friend. Use a separate piece of paper for your paragraph.

1. Wie ist er/sie? (glücklich, laut, leise, (un)kompliziert, usw.)
2. Was hat er/sie gern? Was sind seine/ihre Interessen und Aktivitäten? Was hat er/sie? (Radio, Fernseher, Fahrrad, usw.)

Copyright © 1989 by Holt, Rinehart and Winston, Inc. All rights reserved.

KAPITEL 3 WAS ICH BIN, WOHER ICH KOMME UND WOHIN ICH GEHE

PART ONE

I. UND SIE?

A. Woher kommen sie? Five people were interviewed for German television at the **Frankfurter Messe** (Frankfurt Trade Fair). Listen to what the interpreters say about each person and decide the country of his or her nationality. Write in English the name of the country. You will hear each passage twice.

BEISPIEL Ich bin Engländerin, aber ich spreche auch Deutsch und Italienisch. Mein Vater arbeitet in Italien und ich besuche ihn oft.

Beispiel **England**

1. _____ 2. _____

3. _____ 4. _____

5. _____

Copyright © 1989 by Holt, Rinehart and Winston, Inc. All rights reserved.

Speaking a second language opens professional chances

 # Zweisprachigkeit verbessert die Berufschancen

B. Wir brauchen ein Hotelzimmer! Help the director of a large tour group make hotel room assignments by listening to the taped information about tour participants. Indicate each person's sex and profession by marking your answer sheet according to the example. You will hear each person's description twice.

BEISPIEL   B. Jahn, 42, Berliner, Polizist

		MALE	FEMALE	PROFESSION
Beispiel	B. Jahn, 42	✓	_____	Policeman
1.	L. Lundt, 22	_____	_____	_____
2.	U. Meier, 30	_____	_____	_____
3.	M. Tannenberg, 45	_____	_____	_____
4.	F. Bermann, 30	_____	_____	_____
5.	N. Neuner, 32	_____	_____	_____
6.	W. Fröhlich, 40	_____	_____	_____

C. Ist das richtig? Beate and Ulf are preparing name tags for a large conference. Some of the name tags have mistakes on them so they have asked you to check the registration forms for the correct information. Use the information on the registration forms to answer their questions.

BEISPIEL   Ist Herr Levenson Amerikaner?
        Nein, er ist Kanadier.

Copyright © 1989 by Holt, Rinehart and Winston, Inc. All rights reserved.

International Conference on Environmental Concerns

June 8-11, 1989
Basel, Switzerland

Name Harry Levenson   Age 42

Occupation/Profession Computer specialist

Address   2425 Queen's Highway

       Toronto, Ontario, Canada

International Conference on Environmental Concerns

June 8-11, 1989
Basel, Switzerland

Name François Le Boeuf   Age 43

Occupation/Profession Scientist, CEBA

Address Basel, Switzerland

International Conference on Environmental Concerns

June 8-11, 1989
Basel, Switzerland

Name Friedrich W. Engelmann   Age 33

Occupation/Profession Waiter

Address Hotel Europa, Neuer Markt/Kärntnerstraße

       Vienna, Austria

International Conference on Environmental Concerns

June 8-11, 1989
Basel, Switzerland

Name Sheila F. Johnston   Age 28

Occupation/Profession Engineer, XYZ Consulting

Address Northampton, England

---

1   2   3   4   5   6

Copyright © 1989 by Holt, Rinehart and Winston, Inc. All rights reserved.

35

II. AUSSPRACHE

A. The following consonant sounds exist in both German and English, but their spelling is not always the same. Listen to the tape, then repeat these words. Pay particular attention to their spellings.

/f/	für fleißig Fenster Beruf viel von Vater aktiv Verkäufer
/v/	wir was warum Wien wiedersehen wichtig Krankenschwester Schweiz
/z/	so seit sehr sauber sagen sein sechzehn Musik reisen organisiert besuchen
/s/	es das groß Haus aus realistisch ernst Großeltern Grüße
/ts/	Magazin kompliziert Pflanze siebzehn Katze ganz zu Zeit zufrieden Zimmer ziemlich

B. Repeat the following words.

/t/	Tag Stadt nett Thomas Theater Hund gesund Kind Geld
/t/—/d/	Hund—Hunde England—Engländer Kind—Kinder Rad—Räder Geld—Gelder Bild—Bilder Freund—Freundin Wand—Wände
/g/	gut Geld gehen Angelika aggressiv Berge Tage
/k/	Klavier Onkel glücklich genug Berg Tag
/k/—/g/	Tag—Tage Berg—Berge sag'—sagen frag'—fragen
/b/	bitte bist Beruf schreiben Problem
/p/	Platte Camping Computer Schreibmaschine lieb hab'
/p/—/b/	lieb—lieber hab'—haben

Repeat the following sentences.

1. Vas sagst du, Großvater? //
2. ele fleißige Verkäufer arbeiten seit siebzehn Tagen in Wien. //
3. M. 'n Zimmer ist ziemlich sauber und organisiert. //
4. De. Engländer bringt sein Rad und seinen Hund von England nach Kar. la. //

III. BA 'STEIN 3.1: MÖCHTE

A. . . . **und Funktion** *(Kein Job für mich!)*

B. Was möchten sie? Listen as the following people tell what they or others would like to be, become, or do. For each sentence you hear, put a check mark under the column that best corresponds to what they are saying. Each sentence will be read twice.

Copyright © 1989 by Holt, Rinehart and Winston, Inc. All rights reserved.

BEISPIEL   Ich möchte Arzt werden.

	BE	**BECOME**	**DO (action)**
Beispiel	_____	____✓____	_____
1.	_____	_____	_____
2.	_____	_____	_____
3.	_____	_____	_____
4.	_____	_____	_____
5.	_____	_____	_____
6.	_____	_____	_____

*C. Berufswechsel.   (Career change.) A group of people are attending a seminar on changing careers. Use the cues to tell what they say.

BEISPIEL   Mein Mann ist Mechaniker. (teacher)
          Mein Mann ist Mechaniker, aber er möchte Lehrer werden.

1   2   3   4   5   6

IV.   BAUSTEIN 3.2: DATIVE CASE OF INDIRECT OBJECTS

A. . . . und Funktion *(Fragen, Fragen!)*

B. Der G'schaftlhuber.   (The busybody.) Arnold is always poking into other people's business. Listen to how his friends respond, and decide if the indirect object in each response is a noun or a pronoun. Indicate your answer by putting a check mark in the appropriate column. You will hear each exchange twice.

BEISPIEL   Wem schickst du das Paket?
          Ich schicke es meinem Freund.

	NOUN	**PRONOUN**
Beispiel	____✓____	_____
1.	_____	_____
2.	_____	_____

Copyright © 1989 by Holt, Rinehart and Winston, Inc. All rights reserved.   **37**

3. _____ _____

4. _____ _____

5. _____ _____

*B. Reisegeschenke. (Travel gifts.) Just back from an international conference, Gabi is showing her friend Bettina some of the souvenirs she bought. Give Gabi's answers to Bettina's questions.

BEISPIEL   Wem gibst du den Kugelschreiber? (meine Mutter)
Ich gebe meiner Mutter den Kugelschreiber.

1   2   3   4   5   6

*C. In München.   In his job as a tour guide, Rolf is always willing to show people around. Tell how Rolf responds to what the receptionist says to him.

BEISPIEL   Die Lehrerin möchte das Museum sehen.
Ich zeige es ihr.

1   2   3   4   5   6

V. BAUSTEIN 3.3: DATIVE PREPOSITIONS

A. . . . und Funktion *(Beim Zoll.)*

B. Bei der Konferenz.   The following excerpts from conversations were overheard at a social hour during an international conference. Underline the letter of the phrase that best completes each statement about what was said. You will hear each conversation twice.

BEISPIEL   Frau Klinger, das ist Max Stern. Herr Stern arbeitet in Freilassing, einer Stadt bei Salzburg, aber er wohnt in Berchtesgaden. Freut mich, Herr Stern.

Beispiel Mr. Stern works in . . .
    a.   a town near Salzburg
    b.   Salzburg
    c.   a town near Berchtesgaden
1.   Which of the following statements is most accurate?
    a. Because Ms. Mayer is in the United States, she is working as an interpreter.

Copyright © 1989 by Holt, Rinehart and Winston, Inc. All rights reserved.

38

b. Ms. Mayer has been an interpreter for three years.

c. For the last three years she has been working as an interpreter in the United States.

2. The speakers in this conversation are talking about . . .

a. going to a conference to see a film.

b. going to see a film after the conference.

c. seeing a film at the conference.

3. In this exchange you heard that Mr. Schmidt . . .

a. brought his family along because the hotel was inexpensive.

b. is staying in the hotel with his family.

c. is renting a room with a family because the rooms at the hotel are too expensive.

*C. Reisepläne. (Travel plans.) Several young people are getting acquainted at an international youth conference. Use the cues to tell where each of them is from and where they are traveling next.

BEISPIEL Alois: München — Italien
Alois kommt aus München und reist nach Italien.

Luise: die Bundesrepublik — die Schweiz
Luise kommt aus der Bundesrepublik und reist in die Schweiz.

1   2   3   4   5   6   7   8

VI. BAUSTEIN 3.4: VERBS WITH THE DATIVE

A. . . . und Funktion *(Im Zug.)*

B. Was ist los? (What's the matter?) Several people have been stranded in the Frankfurt airport because their flight was delayed. They are tired and angry, and things are starting to go wrong. For each sentence or exchange you hear, decide whether a dative verb or preposition is present. If you hear a dative verb or preposition, put a check mark in the column marked "dative"; if you do not hear a dative, mark "none". You will hear each item twice.

BEISPIEL   Sie antworten mir nicht!

	DATIVE	NONE
Beispiel	✓	
1.		
2.		

Copyright © 1989 by Holt, Rinehart and Winston, Inc. All rights reserved.

3. _____ _____

4. _____ _____

5. _____ _____

6. _____ _____

7. _____ _____

8. _____ _____

*C. Wem gehört was? A group of students has returned from an outing, and two of them are trying to sort out the items they took along. What do they say?

BEISPIEL Wem gehört die Gitarre? (ich)
Die Gitarre gehört mir.

1   2   3   4   5   6

*D. Wie gefällt ihnen das? Frau Koch is on a tour. A person in her travel group keeps asking her how she and others like things. How does Frau Koch answer?

BEISPIEL Wie gefällt Herrn Schmidt der Dom? (sehr gut)
Er gefällt ihm sehr gut.

1   2   3   4   5   6

VII. SYNTHESE

A. Ich möchte . . . The Schlegels are entering a "dream contest" and hope to win the grand prize of 500,000 Marks. They are submitting a tape in which each family member tells the things he or she would most like. Take brief notes in German as the family members talk, writing down only the key words to help you remember what each person wants. Each segment will be read twice. After each segment, stop the tape and use your notes to write two complete sentences about what each person would like.

BEISPIEL Ich bin Großmutter Schlegel. Hm . . . ich möchte nicht viel. Ich bin alt und brauche keine Motorräder oder Autos. Ich möchte aber ein Fahrrad haben . . . für meinen Sohn natürlich. Ich möchte auch genug Geld für eine Schreibmaschine.

Copyright © 1989 by Holt, Rinehart and Winston, Inc. All rights reserved. **40**

BEISPIEL   Großmutter Schlegel: (1) _*Fahrrad — Sohn*_
          (2) _*Geld für Schreibmaschine*_
          (a) **Sie möchte ein Fahrrad für ihren Sohn.**
          (b) **Sie möchte auch genug Geld für eine Schreibmaschine.**

Was möchten die Schlegels?

Johann Schlegel: (1) _____ (2) _____

a. _____

b. _____

Naomi Schlegel: (1) _____ (2) _____

a. _____

b. _____

Uschi Schlegel: (1) _____ (2) _____

a. _____

b. _____

B. Gute Reise!   Imagine you are to recommend good vacation spots abroad for the following people. Give your recommendations in complete sentences at the sound of the tone.

BEISPIEL   Für einen Spanischprofessor . . .
          Für einen Spanischprofessor, eine Reise nach Mexiko.

1. Für einen Arbeiter aus Detroit . . .
2. Für einen Tierarzt aus der DDR . . .
3. Für eine Engländerin aus Manchester . . .
4. Für Menschen aus New York City . . .
5. Für eine Flugpilotin aus Kalifornien . . .
6. Für mich . . .

Copyright © 1989 by Holt, Rinehart and Winston, Inc. All rights reserved.

PART TWO

I. BAUSTEIN 3.1: <u>MÖCHTE</u>

A. Was möchten Sie? Use a form of **möchten** to describe what the people in the following illustrations would like to do or be.

BEISPIEL **Sie möchte Computertechnikerin werden.**

1. _____

_____

Copyright © 1989 by Holt, Rinehart and Winston, Inc. All rights reserved.

2. _____

_____

3. _____

_____

Copyright © 1989 by Holt, Rinehart and Winston, Inc. All rights reserved.

4. _____

_____

5. _____

_____

Copyright © 1989 by Holt, Rinehart and Winston, Inc. All rights reserved.

6. _____

_____

7. _____

_____

Copyright © 1989 by Holt, Rinehart and Winston, Inc. All rights reserved.

8. _____

_____

B. Imagine yourself on a perfect day. List five things you would like to do or be.

BEISPIEL   **Ich möchte Wien besuchen.**

1. _____

2. _____

3. _____

4. _____

5. _____

Copyright © 1989 by Holt, Rinehart and Winston, Inc. All rights reserved.

II. BAUSTEIN 3.2: DATIVE CASE OF INDIRECT OBJECTS

A. Wer macht was? Choosing from the words and pictures, write meaningful sentences with both direct and indirect objects. Then rewrite the sentences, substituting pronouns for noun objects according to the model.

BEISPIEL: Der Hund bringt dem Mann die Zeitung.
Der Hund bringt ihm die Zeitung.
Der Hund bringt sie ihm.

1. _____

_____

_____

Copyright © 1989 by Holt, Rinehart and Winston, Inc. All rights reserved.

2. _____

_____

_____

3. _____

_____

_____

Copyright © 1989 by Holt, Rinehart and Winston, Inc. All rights reserved.

4. _____

_____

_____

5. _____

_____

_____

Copyright © 1989 by Holt, Rinehart and Winston, Inc. All rights reserved.

B. Wer, wem oder was? For each of the sentences you wrote in **A**, form two questions using the interrogatives **wer, wem,** or **was.**

BEISPIEL   Wer bringt dem Mann die Zeitung?   or
Wem bringt der Hund die Zeitung?   or
Was bringt der Hund dem Mann?

1. _____

_____

2. _____

_____

3. _____

_____

4. _____

_____

5. _____

_____

III. BAUSTEIN 3.3: DATIVE PREPOSITIONS

A. Ein Briefwechsel. Maria is introducing herself to a new pen pal in Canada. Choose from the following prepositions to complete her sentences.

bei	für	nach	gegen	durch
mit	ohne	außer	von	zu
aus	seit	in	um	

Mein Name ist Maria Kast. Ich komme _____ der Bundes-

republik und wohne in einer kleinen Stadt _____ Frankfurt.

Meine Eltern sind Lehrer _____ Beruf. Sie haben _____

Copyright © 1989 by Holt, Rinehart and Winston, Inc. All rights reserved.

mir noch eine Tochter. Sie heißt Elenore und wohnt _____ zwei

Jahren nicht mehr _____ Hause. Sie ist jetzt Dolmetscherin und

fährt oft _____ Kanada und _____ die Vereinigten

Staaten. Das finde ich toll, denn ich reise auch sehr gern. Ich möchte das

nächste Mal (*the next time*) _____ ihr _____ New York

fahren. Elenore ist aber _____ meinen Plan. Sie sagt, ich bin zu

jung _____ eine Reise über den Atlantischen Ozean! Ich denke, sie

fährt einfach (*simply*) lieber _____ ihre ,,kleine'' Schwester!

B. Die neue Zimmerkameradin.

Sigrid is asking Kirsten questions to find out how they would get along as roommates. Complete her questions by giving the appropriate equivalents of the words in parentheses.

1. Hast du keine Pflanzen _____?

   (*besides your cactus*)

2. Wohnst du lieber hier oder _____?

   (*at your grandparents' house*)

3. Du kommst _____ Hannover, nicht wahr?

   (*from a city near*)

4. Fährst du oft _____ Hannover _____ Eltern?

   (*to/to your*)

5. Bist du gern _____?

   (*with friends*)

Copyright © 1989 by Holt, Rinehart and Winston, Inc. All rights reserved.

6. _____ sind die Platten? *(From whom)*

7. Kommst du oft spät _____? *(home)*

8. Ich esse gern in dem italienischen Restaurant

   _____, du auch?

   (across from the university)

9. Ich bin gern _____, du auch? *(at home)*

10. Ich bin _____ Studentin, und du?

    (r two years)

BAUSTEIN 3.4: VERBS WITH THE DATIVE

.. Die Zollbeamtin. (Customs official.) Heinz and Max are returning to Switzerland after a trip to the United States. Complete the dialogue between them and the customs official by filling in the appropriate pronouns.

1. Zollbeamtin: ,,Gehören _____ der Koffer und das Paket?''

   Heinz: ,,Wie bitte? Schöner Tag, nicht wahr?''

2. Zollbeamtin: ,,Warum antworten Sie _____ nicht? Gehört

   _____ der Koffer?''

   Heinz: ,,Nein, er gehört _____!'' (Er zeigt auf seinen Freund.)

   Max: ,,Was? Der Koffer gehört _____, Heinz.''

3. Zollbeamtin: ,,Meine Herren, bitte! Das gefällt _____ nicht!

   Ich bin Zollbeamtin. Was haben Sie im Koffer?''

   Heinz: ,,Absolut nichts. Na ja, Parfüm für meine Frau, Schokolade für

   meine Kinder und Wein für meine Freunde. Geschenke gefallen

   _____.''

Copyright © 1989 by Holt, Rinehart and Winston, Inc. All rights reserved.

4. Zollbeamtin: „Aha! Absolut nichts, sagen Sie. Ich glaube

_____ nicht. Zeigen Sie _____ den Koffer bitte.

Ich helfe _____.“

Heinz: „Ach ja, O.K., ich danke _____.“

B. Wem gefällt was (nicht)? Complete the following sentences by choosing objects from the balloon, or by supplying your own.

BEISPIEL   Langweilige Städte gefallen den Touristen nicht.
 Eine komplizierte Hausaufgabe gefällt mir.

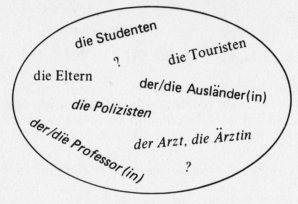

die Studenten
?
die Touristen
die Eltern
der/die Ausländer(in)
die Polizisten
der/die Professor(in)
der Arzt, die Ärztin
?

1. Schnelle Autos _____

2. Schnellrestaurants _____

3. Meine Stereoanlage _____

4. Eine komplizierte Hausaufgabe _____

5. Faule Studenten _____

6. Gesunde Menschen _____

V. SYNTHESE

A. Ein Telegramm von Freunden. Imagine that you have received the following telegram from friends who are on vacation. In the space provided, write out in complete and meaningful sentences your friends' message.

Copyright © 1989 by Holt, Rinehart and Winston, Inc. All rights reserved.   **54**

Telegramm	**Deutsche Bundespost**	Verzögerungsvermerke		
Datum Uhrzeit	Empfangen von	Leitvermerk	Datum Uhrzeit	
Empfangen			Gesendet	
Platz Namenszeichen			Platz Namenszeichen	

Bezeichnung der Aufgabe-TSt	Aufgabe-Nr.	Wortzahl	Aufgabetag	Uhrzeit	Via/Leitweg

aus

Die stark umrahmten Teile sind vom Absender auszufüllen. Bitte Rückseite beachten.

Gebührenpflichtige Dienstvermerke

=   =

Name des Empfängers, Straße, Hausnummer usw.

Michael May, Hauptstraße 65, 3550 Hierstadt, BRD

Bestimmungsort – Bestimmungs-TSt

Stuttgart, Hauptpost

SIND BEI FREUNDEN AUS USA. REISEN MORGEN SCHWEIZ. FLIEGEN DANN

ZÜRICH/MADRID. MIT ZUG DANN BARCELONA. FINDEN REISE TOLL.

KARL UND LOLA

Copyright © 1989 by Holt, Rinehart and Winston, Inc. All rights reserved.

B. Ich möchte ein Telegramm schicken.   Imagine that you are on
vacation and want to send friends a telegram in German. To whom
would you send the telegram? Would the message be funny or serious?
Use complete sentences to create the draft for a short telegram.

_____

_____

_____

_____

Now write your message in "telegram style." Remember that you pay for
each word, but that your message must be comprehensible to the recipient.

_____

_____

_____

_____

C. Ferienpläne.   Using the following questions as a guide, write a
paragraph planning a vacation trip abroad. Use a separate piece of
paper for your paragraph.

Mit wem machen Sie die Reise? (Freunden, Geschwister, Bruder, Eltern?)
Oder fahren Sie allein?
Wie fahren Sie? (mit dem Schiff, fliegen?)
Wohin fahren Sie? (BRD, DDR, Schweiz, Italien, Sowjetunion, Kanada?)
Wie sparen Sie Geld für die Reise?
Wem kaufen Sie Geschenke?

Copyright © 1989 by Holt, Rinehart and Winston, Inc. All rights reserved.

KAPITEL 4 UNTERWEGS
PART ONE

I. UND SIE?

Ich bin fremd hier. (I'm new in town.) Listen to the following conversations as people who are new in town ask for directions to various places. For each conversation you hear, underline the name of the place these people are trying to find. You will hear each conversation twice.

BEISPIEL   Entschuldigung, können Sie mir sagen, wo die nächste Bank ist?
Hm . . . Ich glaube in der Nähe vom Bahnhof. Fahren Sie doch mit der U-Bahn bis zum Bahnhof.

Beispiel a. bank   b. train station   c. money exchange   d. subway
1. a. church   b. newsstand   c. department store   d. train station
2. a. museum   b. movie theater   c. parking lot   d. newsstand
3. a. youth hostel   b. hotel   c. post office   d. marketplace
4. a. university   b. church   c. museum   d. subway
5. a. department store   b. cathedral   c. restaurant   d. hotel
6. a. town hall   b. streetcar   c. subway   d. train station

II. AUSSPRACHE

Listen to the tape, then practice the following consonant sounds. Notice their spellings.

A.

/ç/   i**ch** ni**ch**t ziemli**ch** Österrei**ch** Kir**ch**e Grie**ch**e **Ch**emie
Re**ch**tsanwalt mö**ch**te lebendi**g** trauri**g** ri**ch**ti**g**
/x/   brau**ch**en au**ch** na**ch** a**ch** ma**ch**en

Copyright © 1989 by Holt, Rinehart and Winston, Inc. All rights reserved.

B.

/ʃ/	**sch**ön Ent**sch**uldigung **sch**nell **Sch**wimmbad **sch**icken typi**sch** Men**sch** realisti**sch**
/ʃt/	**St**raße **St**adt **St**udent
/ʃp/	**Sp**ort **Sp**aß **sp**rechen **Sp**iel
/st/	Po**st** Re**st**aurant In**st**rument Kun**st** reali**st**isch

C. Practice pronouncing the following sentences.

1. Ach, ich brauche dich nicht.
2. Die Studenten stehen vor der Post und sprechen über Sport und Spiele.

III. BAUSTEIN 4.1: IMPERATIVES

A. . . . und Funktion *(Wie komme ich zu . . . ?)*

B. Pfadfinderfest. (Boy scout jamboree.) Herr Hochwasser is taking a group of **Pfadfinder** on a weekend trip to the **Bodensee.** For each thing you hear him tell the boy scouts to do, decide whether he's talking to one or more than one of them. Put a check mark in the appropriate column. You will hear each sentence twice.

BEISPIEL   Helft mir mit den Fahrrädern!

	ONE	MORE THAN ONE
Beispiel	_____	____✓____
1.	_____	_____
2.	_____	_____
3.	_____	_____
4.	_____	_____
5.	_____	_____
6.	_____	_____

C. Im Informationsamt. Herr Schmidt, an employee at the information center in Frankfurt, is giving directions to various tourists. What does he say?

Copyright © 1989 by Holt, Rinehart and Winston, Inc. All rights reserved.

BEISPIEL   hier warten
          Warten Sie hier!

1   2   3   4   5

IV.   BAUSTEIN 4.2: TWO-WAY PREPOSITIONS

A. . . . und Funktion *(Mach schnell!)*

B. Familienurlaub.   The Hess family is getting ready for their annual vacation. Listen to what each person says, and decide whether the preposition in the sentence requires the dative or the accusative case. Put a check mark in the appropriate column to indicate your choice. You will hear each sentence twice.

BEISPIEL   Mutti, fahren wir aufs Land?

	ACCUSATIVE	DATIVE
Beispiel	✓	
1.		
2.		
3.		
4.		
5.		
6.		

C. Wo oder wohin?   Anneliese Beck is leading a **Globus** tour of Mainz and is answering questions before the tourists get off the bus. For each answer you hear, give the question the tourist probably asked. Begin your questions with either **wo** or **wohin.**

BEISPIEL   Wir übernachten im Europahotel.
          Wo übernachten wir?

1   2   3   4   5   6

Copyright © 1989 by Holt, Rinehart and Winston, Inc. All rights reserved.

V. BAUSTEIN 4.3: DAYS, MONTHS, SEASONS

A. . . . und Funktion *(Kommst du auch?)*

B. Der Kalender.   It's Monday, June 1st, and Mrs. Brown is putting her calendar in order for the next two weeks. Listen as she reads some of the notes her German housekeeper Hedwig has left on the desk. Write key words in English under the appropriate days to remind her what she is supposed to do then. You will hear each message twice.

BEISPIEL   Gehen Sie dieses Wochenende ins Kino!

			JUNE			
SUN	MON	TUES	WED	THUR	FRI	SAT
	1	2	3	4	5	6 *go to movies*
7 *go to movies*	8	9	10	11	12	13
14	15	16	17	18	19	20

1   2   3   4   5

*C. Wann?   The members of the **Hamburger Kulturverein** (Culture Society) are scheduling future meetings. Give the members' answers to the questions that are asked.

BEISPIEL   Wann fahrt ihr in die Stadt? (am Samstag)
         Wir fahren am Samstag in die Stadt.

1   2   3   4   5   6   7   8

Copyright © 1989 by Holt, Rinehart and Winston, Inc. All rights reserved.   **60**

VI. BAUSTEIN 4.4: WORD ORDER

A. . . . und Funktion *(Im Reisebüro.)*

B. Besuch mich doch!   Irene is talking to a friend on the phone, encouraging him to visit her in Basel. Listen to what she says, paying particular attention to the position of the conjugated verb in each sentence. Put a check mark in the column that best describes the word order used. You will hear each sentence twice.

BEISPIEL   Du fragst mich, was man in Basel am Wochenende macht.

	VERB FIRST	SIMPLE SENTENCE: VERB SECOND	VERB LAST
Beispiel	_____	_____	✓ _____
1.	_____	_____	_____
2.	_____	_____	_____
3.	_____	_____	_____
4.	_____	_____	_____
5.	_____	_____	_____
6.	_____	_____	_____

*C. Ich höre . . .   Amy has just returned from a trip to Austria, and Morris would like her to tell him more about the country and people. Use the cues to tell what Morris says.

BEISPIEL   Es gibt in Wien viele Cafés.
        Ich höre, daß es in Wien viele Cafés gibt.

1   2   3   4   5   6

VII. SYNTHESE

A. Richtig oder falsch?   Listen as a pedestrian gives Jakob Lutz information about certain places. Look at the map and locate these places from your perspective. Indicate **richtig** if the information is

Copyright © 1989 by Holt, Rinehart and Winston, Inc. All rights reserved.

correct, and **falsch** if the information is incorrect. You will hear each sentence twice.

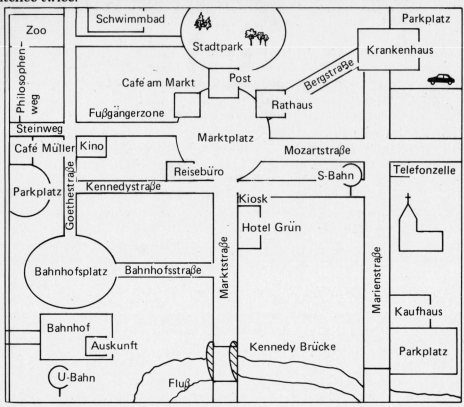

Auskunft = Information

1. richtig falsch   2. richtig falsch   3. richtig falsch
4. richtig falsch   5. richtig falsch   6. richtig falsch

B. Wie kommt man zu . . . ? Listen as directions are given to an undisclosed place. The passage will be read twice. During the first reading, take brief notes; the second time, follow the trail on the map from activity **A**. At the end of the tape you will learn the destination.

Notizen: _____

_____

_____

_____

Wo sind Sie? _____

Copyright © 1989 by Holt, Rinehart and Winston, Inc. All rights reserved.

PART TWO

I. BAUSTEIN 4.1: IMPERATIVES

A. Gute Ratschläge.   (Good advice.) Amanda and Adam are planning a trip to **Wien**, where they will stay with Austrian families. Their
friends are making lots of suggestions. Choose from the following
verbs to complete their statements.

VERBEN: **geben, sprechen, sein, helfen, beantworten, bringen,
schicken, essen, kaufen**

1. Adam, _____ deiner österreichischen Familie ein

    Geschenk aus den Vereinigten Staaten!

2. Amanda, _____ immer Deutsch mit deiner österrei-

    chischen Familie!

3. Adam und Amanda, _____ immer freundlich und nett!

4. Adam, _____ dem Sohn in deiner Familie mit seinem

    Englisch!

5. Amanda, _____ nicht zu viele Wiener Spezialitäten!

6. Amanda und Adam, _____ uns viele Bilder von euren

    Familien!

7. Amanda und Adam, _____ immer unsere Briefe!

8. Adam, _____ einer Österreicherin meine Adresse. Ich

    möchte eine Brieffreundin im Ausland haben!

Copyright © 1989 by Holt, Rinehart and Winston, Inc. All rights reserved.   **63**

Jeder Urlaub hat seinen Bahnhof.
Wohin Sie auch fahren möchten, in die Berge oder an die See oder
. . . oder in den Wald. Die Bahn fährt Sie hin.
DEUTSCHE BUNDESBAHN [DB]

B. Was denken Sie? An Austrian friend is planning a summer trip to the United States. Using the model as a guide, indicate whether you agree or disagree with your friend's plans.

BEISPIEL Ich möchte New York besuchen.
Besuch nicht New York! Es ist dort zu teuer.
Besuch New York! Die Stadt ist sehr interessant und lebendig.

1. Ich fahre mit dem Zug nach Kalifornien.

_____

2. Ich möchte eine Reise nach Florida machen.

_____

3. Ich fliege von Chicago nach Detroit.

_____

4. Ich möchte im Mississippifluß schwimmen.

_____

5. Ich möchte immer in Jugendherbergen übernachten.

_____

6. Ich möchte in einem Schnellrestaurant arbeiten.

_____

II. BAUSTEIN 4.2: TWO-WAY PREPOSITIONS

A. In der Auskunft. The information bureau in Frankfurt is a busy place. Describe what is going on by completing each sentence below

Copyright © 1989 by Holt, Rinehart and Winston, Inc. All rights reserved.

with the appropriate preposition and definite or indefinite article or possessive adjective.

PRÄPOSITIONEN: **an, auf, hinter, in, neben, über, unter, vor, zwischen**

1. Herr and Frau Meisel kommen _____ Zimmer.

2. Eine Pflanze steht _____ Tür.

3. Fräulein Machtel sitzt _____ Schreibtisch.

4. Klaus wartet _____ Schreibtisch.

5. Klaus steht _____ Amerikaner und _____

   Österreicherin.

6. Joans Koffer steht _____ Tisch.

Copyright © 1989 by Holt, Rinehart and Winston, Inc. All rights reserved. **65**

7. Frau Lange sitzt _____ Stuhl und wartet _____

Familie.

8. Mr. Shelton liest _____ Restaurants in Frankfurt.

B. Wo und wohin? Joanne has just arrived in **Luzern** and is talking to her Swiss friend, Robi, on the telephone. You hear only Joanne's side of the conversation, so fill in what Robi might be saying.

1. Joanne: Du hast jetzt keine Zeit? Wohin gehst du denn?

   Robi: _____

2. Joanne: Ja? Wie schön. Ich möchte auch einen Film sehen. Wo ist das Kino?

   Robi: _____

3. Joanne: Aber wo ist das? Ich bin fremd hier!

   Robi: _____

4. Joanne: Langsam, bitte. Hinter was? Und zwischen was?

   Robi: _____

5. Joanne: Aha. Und wo nehme ich den Bus? Und wohin fährt er?

   _____

6. Joanne: Ja gut. Und was machen wir nach dem Film?

   Robi: _____

III. BAUSTEIN 4.3: DAYS, MONTHS, SEASONS

A. Unterwegs. Frau Ehrlich is telling when members of her family go to various places. Recreate her statements by filling in the blanks of the following sentences with the appropriate days of the week, month, or season. Create appropriate expressions by combining elements from the two columns listed.

Copyright © 1989 by Holt, Rinehart and Winston, Inc. All rights reserved.

BEISPIEL   Wir gehen **jeden Mittwoch** zur Post.

am	Herbst
im	Woche
nächste	Sommer
nächsten	Jahr
diese	Winter
diesen	Montag (Dienstag usw.)
dieses	Wochenende
jede	Frühling
jeden	Januar (Februar, März usw.)
jedes	Monat
	Tag

Jeden
Dienstag   **Flohmarkt**

**Freiburger
Nachrichten**

in den

1. Wir fahren _____ ifs Land.

2. Ich mache _____ eine Geschäftsreise

    nach Paris.

3. Mein Mann fliegt _____ in die Vereinigten

    Staaten.

4. Rolf besucht _____ seine Freundin in

    Düsseldorf.

5. Meine Schwester Sabine reist _____ nach

    Hamburg.

6. Mein Mann und ich wandern _____ in

    den Bergen.

Copyright © 1989 by Holt, Rinehart and Winston, Inc. All rights reserved.   **67**

7. Wir alle bleiben lieber _____ zu Hause.

8. Birgit arbeitet _____ in London.

9. Unsere Oma geht _____ zum Schwimm-

bad.

10. Wie Sie sehen, ist unsere Familie _____

sehr aktiv!

B. Und Sie?   Referring to the columns in activity A, create sentences about your activities.

1. Ich möchte <u>am Wochenende</u> _____.

2. _____.

3. _____.

4. _____.

5. _____.

C. Was kann mann . . . machen?   (What can you do . . . ?) Complete the following expressions with as many appropriate activities as you can think of.

BEISPIEL   Am Wochenende **reisen**
                          nach Hause fahren
                          in der Bibliothek sitzen
                          _____**?**_____

1. Jeden Montag   _____   _____

                     _____   _____

                     _____   _____

                     _____   _____

Copyright © 1989 by Holt, Rinehart and Winston, Inc. All rights reserved.

2.   Im Sommer   _____   _____

   _____   _____

   _____   _____

   _____   _____

3.   Nächste Woche   _____   _____

   _____   _____

   _____   _____

   _____   _____

4.   Jeden Tag   _____   _____

   _____   _____

   _____   _____

   _____   _____

IV.   BAUSTEIN 4.4: WORD ORDER

A. Bilden Sie Sätze!   (Form sentences.) Using words and expressions you know, form logical sentences from the following fragments.

BEISPIEL   **Am Wochenende fahren   wir   nach Hause.**

1.   Der Busfahrer weiß, _____

   _____ _____.

2.   Nächstes Jahr _____

   _____ _____.

3.   _____ _____

   _____ ins Theater.

Copyright © 1989 by Holt, Rinehart and Winston, Inc. All rights reserved.

4. Können Sie mir sagen, _____

_____ _____?

5. Manchmal _____ _____

_____ _____.

6. Sie fragt mich, _____

_____ nächste Woche

_____.

B. Ergänzen Sie! (Completions.) Complete sentences 1–6, using question words from the following list.

wohin	woher	daß	weil
was	wie oft	wer	wo
warum	wie	wem	wen

1. Ich möchte wissen, _____.

2. Ich höre, _____.

3. Sie fragt mich, _____.

4. Wissen Sie, _____?

5. Ich mache dieses Jahr keine Reise, _____.

6. Er sagt mir, _____.

C. In der Stadtmitte. A group of tourists has just descended on Vienna. Draw lines connecting components from each column to tell what they might have said.

Wir sind in der Stadtmitte.   Ich habe einen Stadtplan.
Fahren wir mit dem Bus?   Morgen gehe ich mit dir.
Ich habe jetzt keine Zeit.   **und** Wir gehen die Straße entlang.
Ich kenne die Stadt nicht.   **aber** Nehmen wir das Auto?
Fahren wir mit dem Taxi.   **oder** Es ist zu weit für mich.
Du möchtest zu Fuß gehen.   **denn** Die Straßenbahn ist zu langsam.
Ich möchte jetzt essen.   Es gibt um die Ecke ein
                                      Schnellrestaurant.

Copyright © 1989 by Holt, Rinehart and Winston, Inc. All rights reserved.

D. Ausreden, Ausreden. (Excuses, excuses.) In certain situations, it is often necessary to give an excuse. Imagine yourself confronted with the following situations. On the line provided, write the excuse you would give.

BEISPIEL Sie sagen zu Ihren Freunden: ,,Ich gehe mit euch.''
Ich sage, daß ich mit ihnen gehe.

1. Sie sind mit Ihren Freunden bei einer Party. Jetzt möchten Ihre Freunde in eine Disko gehen, aber die Disko gefällt Ihnen gar nicht. Sie finden die Musik zu laut, und die Menschen dort sind nicht sehr nett. Aber Sie haben kein Auto. Sie sagen zu Ihren Freunden:
   a. ,,Am Wochenende gehe ich mit euch, aber nicht heute.''
   b. ,,Ich gehe zu Fuß nach Hause.''
   c. ,,Ich finde die Disko blöd; ich gehe absolut nicht.''
   d.   ?

   _____

2. Am Montag sind Sie immer müde. Nach dem Wochenende ist es schwer für Sie, zur Uni zu gehen und Sie bleiben zu Hause. Später *(later)* sehen Sie Ihre(n) Deutschprofessor(in)! Sie sagen zu ihm/ihr:
   a. ,,Ich habe Deutsch nicht gern.''
   b. ,,Meine Uhr ist kaputt.''
   c. ,,Heute ist mein Geburtstag.''
   d.   ?

   _____

3. Ihre Tante möchte, daß Sie sie am Sonntag besuchen. Sie gehen aber nicht gern, weil es immer so langweilig ist. Sie sagen zu ihr:
   a. ,,Leider habe ich nächsten Sonntag keine Zeit.''
   b. ,,Ich mache am Wochenende eine Reise nach Timbuktu.''
   c. ,,Ich möchte kommen, aber ich habe so viele Hausaufgaben.''
   d.   ?

   _____

4. Ein(e) Freund(in) von Ihnen macht eine Reise in die Bundesrepublik und möchte, daß Sie mit ihm/ihr kommen. Sie reisen aber nicht gern mit ihm/ihr. Sie sagen, Sie gehen nicht mit ihm/ihr, weil:
   a. ,,Ich möchte nicht jeden Tag Deutsch sprechen.''
   b. ,,Ich habe leider keinen Koffer.''
   c. ,,Ich reise nicht gern und bleibe lieber zu Hause.''
   d.   ?

   _____

Copyright © 1989 by Holt, Rinehart and Winston, Inc. All rights reserved.

V. SYNTHESE

A. Entschuldigen Sie . . . Imagine that you are in a German-speaking country. Write an exchange for the following situations.

1. You ask a bystander where the post office is. The bystander says she doesn't know the town very well. She directs you to ask the policeman on the corner. You thank her and say good-bye.

    Sie: _____

    _____

    Frau M.: _____

    _____

    _____

    Sie: _____

2. You think the museum is nearby but you don't know where it is, so you ask someone. He tells you to go straight ahead and to the left, but then he remembers that today is Wednesday, and the museum is not open *(offen)* on Wednesday.

    Sie: _____

    _____

    Herr V.: _____

    _____

    _____

B. Viele Grüße. Imagine you're in Switzerland. Write a postcard to your German Club in the U.S.A. In the space provided, include the following points:

1. Sind Sie in einer Stadt oder auf dem Land?
2. Wo übernachten Sie (Hotel, Jugendherberge, Campingplatz)?
3. Gehen Sie zu Fuß, oder nehmen Sie die Straßenbahn (die U-Bahn, den Bus)?
4. Was machen Sie am Wochenende?

Copyright © 1989 by Holt, Rinehart and Winston, Inc. All rights reserved.

Die schöne Schweiz

Copyright © 1989 by Holt, Rinehart and Winston, Inc. All rights reserved.

KAPITEL 5 BEIM EINKAUFEN

PART ONE

I. UND SIE?

Was braucht ihr? Lisa has volunteered to do the shopping for her housemates. Listen as the following people tell her what to buy while shopping. Recreate her shopping list, including the correct amounts of the items stated. You will hear each request twice.

BEISPIEL   Kaufe bitte ein Kilo Schwarzbrot und ein Stück Käsekuchen in der Bäckerei.

Beispiel   Bakery: **1 kg of rye bread; 1 piece of cheesecake**

Grocery store: _____

_____

Drugstore: _____

_____

Market: _____

_____

Butcher shop: _____

_____

Copyright © 1989 by Holt, Rinehart and Winston, Inc. All rights reserved.

II. AUSSPRACHE

The two basic **r** sounds in German, the uvular /R/ and the tongue-tip trill /r/, are very different from the American **r** sound. Regional, dialectal, and individual differences determine which one will be used.

A. Listen to the tape, then practice the following words. Note how the *r* sound changes in combination with other sounds. /R/ is a voiced uvular trill; /ʁ/ is the unvoiced counterpart.

Rathaus **r**ufen **R**ock **R**eisebüro **r**echts **R**indfleisch
Brücke **Kr**ankenhaus **Br**ot **Fr**äulein **Tr**auben sch**r**eiben St**r**aße
Her**r** p**r**eiswe**r**t Pa**r**k Mä**r**z wa**r**te Jah**r** Janua**r** wah**r** ih**r** Bie**r** hie**r**
seh**r** Tü**r**

B. Contrast and practice the following sounds.

Butt**er** teu**er** dies**er** spät**er** ab**er** Wint**er** Ei**er**
bitte welche Größe Gemüse Hose Seife
welche—welch**er** diese—dies**er** bitte—bitt**er** jede—jed**er**
manche—manch**er**

C. Pronounce the following sentences.

1. Herr und Frau Schneider brauchen Brot, Butter, Bier und Eier.
2. Fräulein Müller trifft eine Freundin vor dem Krankenhaus.
3. Das Bier hier im Rathaus ist teuer.
4. Die Kirche und das Reisebüro sind rechts vor der Brücke.

III. BAUSTEIN 5.1: NUMBERS

A. . . . und Funktion *(Auf dem Markt.)*

B. Im Bahnhof. Kate and Chuck are inquiring about travel distances and the prices for first-class **(erste Klasse)** and second-class **(zweite Klasse)** fares. Help them complete their railway timetable by reconstructing the missing information when it is read by a train official. You will hear each piece of information twice.

BEISPIEL Von Hamburg nach Bremen sind es hundertneunzehn Kilometer. Die Reise kostet siebzehn Mark für zweite Klasse. Die Reise kostet sechsundzwanzig Mark für erste Klasse.

Copyright © 1989 by Holt, Rinehart and Winston, Inc. All rights reserved.

	KILOMETER	2. KLASSE	1. KLASSE
Beispiel Hamburg—Bremen	**119**	DM 17	DM 26
1. Wiesbaden—Essen	_____	DM 38	DM 57
2. Hamburg—Köln	463	DM 67	_____
3. Frankfurt—Nürnberg	238	_____	DM 50
4. Hamburg—München	820	DM 110	_____
5. Bremen—Freiburg	_____	DM 103	DM 155
6. Hannover—Stuttgart	_____	DM 75	DM 113

C. Wo ist es preiswert? The Nagel family is listening to a consumer information program on the radio. Listen as the announcer gives comparison prices for various grocery items at the supermarket and the *Tante Emma Laden*. In the spaces provided, write the amounts and prices you hear. You will hear each item twice.

BEISPIEL   Bananen, ein Kilogramm: Im Supermarkt drei Mark, im Tante Emma Laden 3 Mark 50.

		SUPERMARKT	TANTE EMMA LADEN
Beispiel Bananen:	**1 kg**	DM **3.—**	DM **3,50**
1. Brötchen:	_____	DM_____	DM_____
2. Äpfel:	_____	DM_____	DM_____
3. Milch:	_____	DM_____	DM_____
4. Bier:	_____	DM_____	DM_____
5. Wurst:	_____	DM_____	DM_____
6. Wein:	_____	DM_____	DM_____

Copyright © 1989 by Holt, Rinehart and Winston, Inc. All rights reserved.

*D. Die Telefonnummer ist . . .   An advertising agency is planning to call the following stores. Tell what addresses and telephone numbers the operator would give.

BEISPIEL   Lebensmittelgeschäft Kupsch
Kolpingstr. 509
Tel. 23 76
Kolpingstraße fünfhundertneun.
Die Nummer ist dreiundzwanzig sechsundsiebzig.

1. Metzgerei Meierhof
Baumgartenstr. 48
Tel. 3 20 92

2. Blumengeschäft Grünewald
Hauptstr. 129
Tel. 95 87 71

3. Bäckerei Engel
Baumstr. 343
Tel. 90 65

4. Schuhe Franz
Lindenstr. 278
Tel. 4 89 25

5. Hosen Huber
Bahnhofstr. 53
Tel. 37 44 66

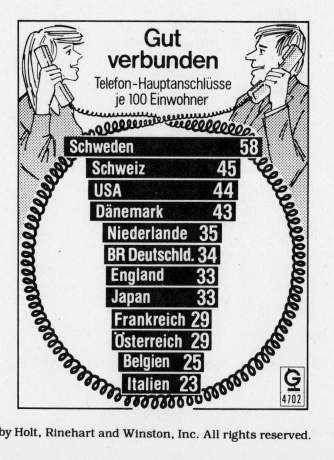

Gut
verbunden
Telefon-Hauptanschlüsse
je 100 Einwohner

Schweden	58
Schweiz	45
USA	44
Dänemark	43
Niederlande	35
BR Deutschld.	34
England	33
Japan	33
Frankreich	29
Österreich	29
Belgien	25
Italien	23

Copyright © 1989 by Holt, Rinehart and Winston, Inc. All rights reserved.

IV. BAUSTEIN 5.2: MODAL VERBS

A. ... und Funktion (*In der Fußgängerzone.*)

B. Eine Reise. Jörg and his father are having a discussion about a trip Jörg and his friends intend to make when school is over. In each of the following conversational exchanges you will hear two modal verbs. Check the columns that correspond to the meanings of the verbs in each exchange. You will hear each exchange twice.

BEISPIEL   Aber Vater, ich will doch meine Freundin mitbringen!
  Das darfst du aber nicht!

	WANT TO	SUPPOSED TO	PERMITTED TO	ABLE TO	MUST, HAVE TO
	✓		✓		
1.					
2.					
3.					
4.					
5.					
6.					
7.					

*C. Was muß ich jetzt machen?   Hans's landlady has asked him to do some errands for her. Using the example as your guide, tell how Hans tells a friend what he must do.

BEISPIEL   Geh zur Bäckerei! Kauf dort ein Schwarzbrot!
  Ich muß zur Bäckerei. Dort soll ich ein Schwarzbrot kaufen.

1   2   3   4   5

*D. Weißt du das?   Renate is talking with a friend about some mutual acquaintances. What does she say?

Copyright © 1989 by Holt, Rinehart and Winston, Inc. All rights reserved.   **79**

BEISPIEL   Johann darf nicht fahren.
           Weißt du, daß Johann nicht fahren darf?

1   2   3   4   5   6   7   8

V.   BAUSTEIN 5.3: SEPARABLE-PREFIX VERBS

A. . . . und Funktion (*Einladung zum Kaffee.*)

B. Im Stadtzentrum.   Lena and Astrid are spending a day down-
town. Listen to some excerpts from their conversations and in each
instance decide if a separable-prefix verb is present. Mark your answer
sheet accordingly. You will hear each sentence twice.

BEISPIEL   Gehen wir doch heute einkaufen!

	YES	**NO**
Beispiel	✓	
1.		
2.		
3.		
4.		
5.		
6.		

C. Warum?   The Hirschhorns think their new friend has been hos-
tile to them, so they've decided to find out why. What do they say? Use
the cues.

BEISPIEL   uns nicht anrufen
           Warum rufst du uns nicht an?

1   2   3   4   5

Copyright © 1989 by Holt, Rinehart and Winston, Inc. All rights reserved.   **80**

Telefonieren ins Ausland ist billiger, als Sie denken.
3 Minuten Frankreich nur 3,45 DM.

Für 1 Minute zahlen Sie etwa DM:

nach	Normaltarif	Billigtarif
Frankreich	1,15	0,92
Großbritannien	1,15	0,92
Portugal	1,15	0,92
USA	3,68	– –

Ruf doch mal an! ✆ Post

*D. So geht's besser! John has thought of several questions to ask, to help him get around in Heidelberg. Judy reminds him that it would be more polite if he prefaced his questions with **Wissen Sie . . . ?** How does John rephrase his questions?

BEISPIEL   Wo soll man anrufen?
          Wissen Sie, wo man anrufen soll?

1   2   3   4   5   6

VI.   BAUSTEIN 5.4: DER-WORDS

A. . . . und Funktion *(Im Kaufhaus.)*

B. Im Kaufhaus.   Klaus is a salesclerk in a department store. He and his supervisor are talking as they take inventory. For each sentence you hear, determine the case of the **der**-word. Put a check mark in the appropriate column. You will hear each sentence twice.

Copyright © 1989 by Holt, Rinehart and Winston, Inc. All rights reserved.

BEISPIEL   Was machen wir mit diesen Hemden?

	NOMINATIVE	ACCUSATIVE	DATIVE
Beispiel	_____	_____	✓
1.	_____	_____	_____
2.	_____	_____	_____
3.	_____	_____	_____
4.	_____	_____	_____
5.	_____	_____	_____
6.	_____	_____	_____

*C. Im Kaufhaus.   Frau Brandt and Frau Pegel are in a department store. Frau Pegel is rather preoccupied today and hears very little of what her friend is saying. What does she ask Frau Brandt to repeat?

BEISPIEL   Dieser Mantel ist preiswert.
           Welcher Mantel ist preiswert?

1   2   3   4   5   6   7   8

VII.   SYNTHESE

A. Kaufen Sie Langleben!   Imagine that you are at a market where a vendor is trying to sell a new brand of tonic called **Langleben.** After listening to what he says, stop the tape and answer the six questions in English. The passage will be read twice.

1.   Why should one try *Langleben?*_____

     _____

2.   Why is *Langleben* healthy for you?_____

     _____

Copyright © 1989 by Holt, Rinehart and Winston, Inc. All rights reserved.

3. What is *Langleben* cheaper than? _____

_____

4. Where can one buy *Langleben*? _____

_____

5. Why should one never be without *Langleben* again? _____

_____

B. Wo kauft man was?   Imagine that a German exchange student
has asked you for advice about where to buy certain things in your
town. Using the list below as a guide, tell your friend where he or she
can buy:

a sweater	fruit
jeans	flowers
a shirt	a gift to send home
fresh meats	

Give reasons for your suggestions, and approximate prices. You may
plan what you will say in the space provided. Begin speaking when
you hear the tone.

_____

_____

_____

_____

_____

_____

Copyright © 1989 by Holt, Rinehart and Winston, Inc. All rights reserved.

PART TWO

I. BAUSTEIN 5.1: NUMBERS

A. Autos. Imagine that you work for an international firm that monitors business trends. You are asked to supply the figures for the five auto manufacturers that improved their market position the most as compared with the previous year. Write out the numbers using the model provided.

Die Auto-Hitliste		
1. VW/Audi	404 818	+ 7,4%
2. Opel	276 319	+ 17,1%
3. Ford	172 154	+ 26,2%
4. Mercedes	132 427	+ 5,4%
5. BMW	90 518	+ 2,3%
6. Fiat	56 832	+ 2,3%
7. Renault	50 331	− 4,2%
8. Mazda	31 284	+ 46,0%
9. Toyota	27 829	+ 30,7%
10. Nissan	24 571	+ 11,3%

BEISPIEL   VW/Audi: **sieben Komma vier Prozent mehr: vierhundertvier-tausendachthundertachtzehn Autos.**

1. _____

   _____

2. _____

   _____

Copyright © 1989 by Holt, Rinehart and Winston, Inc. All rights reserved.

3. _____

_____

4. _____

_____

5. _____

_____

B. Mit dem Scheck zahlen. On vacation Hans finds it more convenient to pay for purchases with a check. Help him complete each check by writing out in full the amounts indicated.

1. Schuhe Vohrer: 210 DM _____

_____

2. Kamerageschäft Kordik: 342 DM _____

_____

3. Kaufhaus Hertie 239 DM _____

_____

4. Hotel Adler: 45 DM _____

_____

5. Büchergeschäft Schulz: 84 DM _____

_____

Copyright © 1989 by Holt, Rinehart and Winston, Inc. All rights reserved.

COMMERZBANK
AKTIENGESELLSCHAFT
HIERSTADT

Zahlen Sie gegen diesen Scheck

Hundertneununundzwanzig

Betrag in Buchstaben

Rosengeschäft Huber

oder Überbringer

Währung	Betrag
DM	129,—

Ort *Bremen*

Datum *11. 7. 84*

Haus Schnüttgen
Unterschrift

Scheck-Nr.	x	Konto-Nr.	x	Betrag	x	Bankleitzahl	x	Text

8901234 5   987654   123456 78 11

Bitte dieses Feld nicht beschriften und nicht bestempeln

C. Im Supermarkt. Imagine you are shopping in Heidelberg with an American friend who knows some German, but needs help with vocabulary for money and measures. Help your friend by translating the English in parentheses.

1. Wieviel kosten _____ (*five hundred grams of cheese*)?

2. Das Gemüse ist frisch, nicht wahr? Geben Sie mir bitte

   _____ (*two kilos of tomatoes*).

3. Acht Brötchen, ein Schwarzbrot und

   _____ (*six pieces of cheesecake*)

   bitte.

4. Geben Sie mir bitte _____ (*four*

Copyright © 1989 by Holt, Rinehart and Winston, Inc. All rights reserved.

cans of cola) und _____ *(two*

bottles of wine).

5. Wieviel kostet _____ *(one pack of*

coffee)?

II. BAUSTEIN 5.2: MODAL VERBS

A. Beim Einkaufen. Several people are discussing shopping in their town. Complete their statements by filling in the blanks with the appropriate form of the modal verbs **können, müssen, dürfen, sollen, wollen,** or **mögen.**

1. In diesem Geschäft ist das Gemüse gar nicht frisch. Ich

    _____ hier nie wieder einkaufen.

2. Der Rock ist mir zu teuer. Ich _____ ihn leider nicht kaufen.

3. Moment mal, ich brauche mehr Geld. _____ ihr mir 50 DM

    geben?

4. Im Café am Markt _____ du nicht rauchen.

5. Mein Mann _____ die Supermärkte nicht. Frisches Gemüse

    und Obst _____ er immer auf dem Markt kaufen.

6. Du _____ Dosenbier kaufen, denn du _____

    nicht so viele Flaschen nach Hause tragen.

B. Was sagen Sie? Write a dialogue based on the situation described below. Feel free to elaborate, but be sure to include modal verbs.

SITUATION   You want to do a certain activity (play tennis/go to a concert/?) and ask a friend whether he/she can come too. Your friend responds that he/she would like to join you, but is supposed to do something else (write letters/do homework/?) You ask whether your friend really has to do these things or whether he/she can do them some other time. Try to convince your friend to forget the other plans and have some fun.

Copyright © 1989 by Holt, Rinehart and Winston, Inc. All rights reserved.   **88**

_____

_____

_____

_____

_____

_____

_____

_____

III.   BAUSTEIN 5.3: SEPARABLE-PREFIX VERBS

A. Eine Party.   Alfons and Christa are getting ready for a big gathering. Using the cues provided, recreate their statements.

BEISPIEL   gehen/schnell/einkaufen//denn/die Geschäfte/zumachen/bald!
   Geh schnell einkaufen, denn die Geschäfte machen bald zu!

1.   anrufen/Volker//und/einladen/ihn/auch/zur Party!

   _____

   _____

2.   Karin/sagen//daß/sie/ihre Platten/mitbringen.

   _____

3.   vielleicht/mitkommen/Marias Freund/auch.
   ich/möchten/ihn/kennenlernen.

   _____

   _____

Copyright © 1989 by Holt, Rinehart and Winston, Inc. All rights reserved.

4. Die Brötchen/sein/nicht frisch.
   zurücknehmen/sie/bitte/zur Bäckerei!

   _____

   _____

B. Ein Wochenende.   Imagine that you are planning a weekend of sightseeing and shopping in a nearby city with friends from your German class. Using the questions below as a guide, write on a separate piece of paper a paragraph detailing your plans.

Wohin fahren Sie? Wer geht mit? Laden Sie Ihre(n) Deutschprofessor(in) auch ein? Lernen Sie viele Leute in der Stadt kennen? Kaufen Sie in den Kaufhäusern ein? Wann fahren Sie zurück? Was bringen Sie zurück?

IV.   BAUSTEIN 5.4: <u>DER-WORDS</u>

A. In der Stadt.   Bob is getting to know Dingskirchen while window-shopping with Gerda. Complete their statements by filling in the blanks with the appropriate form of **dies-, jed-, manch-, solch-, welch-,** or **all-**.

1. Bob: In _____ Geschäft kann man Möbel billig kaufen?

   Gerda: In _____ Kaufhäusern sind die Möbel ziemlich

   preiswert, aber du darfst nicht zu einem Spezialgeschäft für Möbel gehen.

2. Bob: _____ Geschäfte gefallen dir in _____

   Stadt?

   Gerda: Nicht viele, aber _____ Geschäfte am Markt finde

   ich sehr nett.

3. Bob: _____ Geschäft macht um 5 zu!

   Gerda: _____ Geschäft macht zwischen 5 und 6 zu!

4. Bob: Probier doch _____ Schuhe an! Gefallen sie dir?

   Gerda: Nein, _____ Schuhe trage ich nicht!

Copyright © 1989 by Holt, Rinehart and Winston, Inc. All rights reserved.

5. Bob: _____ Einkaufsstraße gefällt mir.

Gerda: Ja, _____ Fußgängerzonen gibt es in vielen Städten.

B. Eine Umfrage. The Chamber of Commerce of a small Austrian town is preparing a survey on consumer attitudes. Translate the following questions, to be put to people on the street.

1. In which grocery stores do you prefer to shop?

    _____

2. Some people find the meat at this market too expensive. And you?

    _____

    _____

3. Which pharmacy do you especially like?

    _____

4. Do you like to shop at this butcher shop?

    _____

5. Do you know every store in this town?

    _____

6. Can one shop inexpensively in such department stores?

    _____

V. SYNTHESE

Werbetexte. (Advertising texts.) For the following ads, write sentences and phrases that would make the products even more appealing to consumers. Write on the blanks and dotted lines provided.

Copyright © 1989 by Holt, Rinehart and Winston, Inc. All rights reserved.

Ist es live – oder ist es MEMOREX

Memtek Products, Dreieichstr. 59, 6 Frankfurt 70

Copyright © 1989 by Holt, Rinehart and Winston, Inc. All rights reserved.

_____

_____

_____

Copyright © 1989 by Holt, Rinehart and Winston, Inc. All rights reserved.

daß . . . .
. . . .

daß . . . .
. . . .

daß . . . .
. . . .

daß . . . .

daß Ihr
Buchhändler viele
in seinem Laden hat und
alle besorgen kann!

**Buchhandlung
Annemarie Tippach**
Petersilienstraße 3 +
Fischemäkerstraße 13
3380 Goslar 1

Copyright © 1989 by Holt, Rinehart and Winston, Inc. All rights reserved.

KAPITEL 6 UM WIEVIEL UHR . . . ?

PART ONE

I. UND SIE?

Im Fernsehstudio. The sound engineer for a television studio is reviewing the audio portion of the day's broadcast. Listen as she plays excerpts from the tape and, in the spaces provided, identify in German the type of program it probably came from. Then, in English, write key words that describe the content of the segment. You will hear each segment twice.

BEISPIEL   Meine Damen und Herren, in unserem Film heute sind wir auf der Reise durch Afrika. Sie sehen wilde Tiere wie Elefanten, Tiger und Giraffen in ihrer natürlichen Umwelt. Also—kommen Sie mit nach Afrika!

	TYPE OF SHOW	KEY WORDS
Beispiel	Dokumentarfilm	trip, Africa, wild animals
1.	_____	_____
2.	_____	_____
3.	_____	_____
4.	_____	_____
5.	_____	_____

Copyright © 1989 by Holt, Rinehart and Winston, Inc. All rights reserved.

II. AUSSPRACHE

A. The German *l* sound is distinctly different from the American "*l*". Listen and then practice the following words, paying particular attention to the *l* sounds.

/l/ Million eigentlich Milch will vielleicht Lebensmittel gefällt schnell Kleid Fleisch leicht Problem Rolf Schule alles Klavier Hallo mal Mantel Apfel manchmal

B. The *schwa* sound /ə/ occurs in unstressed syllables in German. Repeat the following words.

/ə/ beginnen Bericht berühmt habe gesehen Geschichte gefallen geblieben gerade

C. Repeat the following sentences.

1. Rolf will eigentlich schnell berühmt werden.
2. Vielleicht wollen Sie Italienisch lernen.
3. Diese Geschichte beginnt gerade mit einem Bericht.

III. BAUSTEIN 6.1: TELLING TIME; TIME EXPRESSIONS

A. **. . . und Funktion** *(Ich bestehe darauf!)*

B. Stellen Sie die Uhren! (Set the clocks.) As part of their job as building custodians, Herbert and Dieter have been asked to set all the clocks. Complete the digital or standard clock faces on your answer sheet to correspond to the times Herbert announces. You will hear each announcement twice.

Copyright © 1989 by Holt, Rinehart and Winston, Inc. All rights reserved.

NAME _____ DATE _____ CLASS _____

BEISPIEL   Es ist halb sechs.

Beispiel

   or

1.

2.

3.

4.

5.

6.

Copyright © 1989 by Holt, Rinehart and Winston, Inc. All rights reserved.

C. Was gibt's im Fernsehen? Use the information from the TV schedule to answer the questions you hear on the tape. Write your answers in the spaces provided. You will hear each item twice.

Sonntag, 21.

1. Programm

17.45 Heinrich Harrer berichtet
Unter Papuas
Erlebnis Neuguinea
18.30 Tagesschau
18.33 Die Sportschau
Auslosung Tor des Monats; Nordische Skiweltmeisterschaften in Oslo (Springen Normalschanze)
19.15 Wir über uns
19.20 Weltspiegel
20.00 Tagesschau
20.15 Karneval in Köln
Ausschnitte aus der Großen Prunksitzung des Festkomitees des Kölner Karnevals
Regie: Günther Hassert
22.15 Der 7. Sinn
22.20 Tagesschau
22.25 Schlagzeilen
Die ARD-Pressekritik
22.40 Frauen der Welt
Die Herren
Ein Pamphlet gegen die Männerherrschaft von Gordian Troeller und Claude Deffarge
23.25 Tagesschau

2. Programm

17.00 Heute
17.02 Die Sport-Reportage
18.00 Tagebuch
Aus der katholischen Kirche
18.15 Lou Grant
Beginn von zwölf neuen Folgen der TV-Serie
18.58 ZDF — Ihr Programm
19.00 Heute
19.10 Bonner Perspektiven
19.30 Schauplätze der Weltliteratur
Homer und die Ilias
20.15 Der Fall Maurizius (1)
Fernsehfilm in fünf Teilen
Nach dem Roman von Jakob Wassermann
Mit Heinz Bennent, Martin Halm, Sigfrit Steiner, Alice Treff u. a.
Regie: Theodor Kotulla
21.35 Heute, Sport am Sonntag
21.50 Gandhis Welt zerfällt
Aus Indien berichtet Norbert Brieger
22.35 Vom Zauber des Tanzes
Margot Fonteyn erzählt (3)
23.35 Heute

1. _____

2. _____

3. _____

4. _____

D. Die Quizshow. Contestants on a TV game show are asked to talk about various aspects of their daily lives. Listen as each contestant speaks, and then answer the questions on your answer sheet by underlining the correct phrase. You will hear each description twice.

Copyright © 1989 by Holt, Rinehart and Winston, Inc. All rights reserved.

1. Frau Schrader:
   When does Frau Schrader watch TV?
   a. not at all   b. in the afternoon   c. in the evening
2. Herr Gelbert:
   How often does Herr Gelbert shop in a supermarket?
   a. twice a month   b. once a month   c. never
3. Fräulein Macht:
   How often does Fräulein Macht eat lunch at work?
   a. twice a month   b. four times a week   c. three times a week
4. Fräulein Schönfeld:
   When will Fräulein Schönfeld go to the disco alone?
   a. this evening   b. tomorrow evening   c. tomorrow afternoon
5. Herr Fassbinder:
   When does Herr Fassbinder study in the Film Institute Library?
   a. on the weekend   b. in the afternoon   c. in the morning

E. Um wieviel Uhr?   Terry is asking his friend Elmar at what time the Germans usually do certain things. Play the role of Elmar and answer Terry's questions, using the cues you see in your lab manual.

BEISPIEL   Um wieviel Uhr beginnen nachmittags die Kinderprogramme?
           (4.15 Uhr)
           Um vier Uhr fünfzehn.

1. 8.30 Uhr
2. 7.45 Uhr
3. gegen 1.15 Uhr
4. 3.30 Uhr
5. zwischen 12.00 Uhr und 2.00 Uhr
6. von 7.30 Uhr bis 10.30 Uhr

IV. BAUSTEIN 6.2: PRESENT-PERFECT TENSE: IRREGULAR VERBS WITH <u>HABEN</u>

A. . . . und Funktion *(Übers Wochenende.)*

B. Liebe Eltern!   Bettina Jünger is a student at Northwestern University. She has been in the States for about a month and has promised to send her parents a cassette tape. Listen to her tape, and for each verb you hear in the present-perfect tense, write the infinitive in the spaces provided. You will hear the entire tape once, then each sentence individually. Write your responses during the second reading.

Copyright © 1989 by Holt, Rinehart and Winston, Inc. All rights reserved.

BEISPIEL   Meine Freunde hier haben mir mit meinem Englisch geholfen.

Beispiel   __helfen__

1. _____   2. _____

3. _____   4. _____

5. _____   6. _____

*C. Und was hast du heute gemacht?   Irene is telling her friend
Walter some of the things she did during the day. What does she say?
Use the cues indicated.

BEISPIEL   7.00/einen Kaffee trinken
            Um sieben Uhr habe ich einen Kaffee getrunken.

1   2   3   4   5   6   7   8   9   10

*D. Seit wann?   Two friends are getting reacquainted after several
years. Using the cues, give their answers to each other's questions.

BEISPIEL   Wie lange arbeitest du schon bei Hertie? (acht Monate)
            Ich arbeite schon seit acht Monaten bei Hertie.

1   2   3   4   5

V.   BAUSTEIN 6.3: PRESENT-PERFECT TENSE: REGULAR VERBS WITH <u>HABEN</u>

A. . . . und Funktion *(Im Urlaub.)*

B. Skandal!   A controversial television show was aired last night on
Channel 3 and the neighbors are all talking about it. Listen to each
comment and determine whether the verb in the present-perfect tense
is regular, irregular, or mixed. Check the appropriate column. You will
hear each comment twice.

BEISPIEL   Hast du gestern Abend die Sendung gesehen? Schrecklich!

	REGULAR	**IRREGULAR**	**MIXED**
Beispiel	_____	✓	_____
1.	_____	_____	_____

Copyright © 1989 by Holt, Rinehart and Winston, Inc. All rights reserved.

2.   _____   _____   _____

3.   _____   _____   _____

4.   _____   _____   _____

5.   _____   _____   _____

6.   _____   _____   _____

*C. Am Samstag. During dinner, Günther is telling his housemates about his day. What does he say? Use the cues indicated.

BEISPIEL   sehr lange auf die U-Bahn warten
           Ich habe sehr lange auf die U-Bahn gewartet.

1   2   3   4   5   6   7   8   9   10   11

Copyright © 1989 by Holt, Rinehart and Winston, Inc. All rights reserved.

VI. BAUSTEIN 6.4: PRESENT-PERFECT TENSE: VERBS WITH <u>SEIN</u>; PAST TENSE OF <u>SEIN</u>

A. . . . und Funktion *(Wo warst du denn . . . ?)*

B. Zwei Freunde.   Two old friends are getting reacquainted in a café. Listen to what they say and decide for each item whether the speaker is using the present tense or the present-perfect tense. Put a check mark under the correct column. You will hear each item twice.

BEISPIEL   Ich bin mit einem Motorrad durch Italien gereist.

	PRESENT	**PRESENT-PERFECT**
Beispiel	_____	____✓____
1.	_____	_____
2.	_____	_____
3.	_____	_____
4.	_____	_____
5.	_____	_____
6.	_____	_____

*C. Eine Geschäftsreise.   Use the present-perfect tense with **haben** or **sein** to tell what an Austrian businessman did during a recent trip to Munich. Follow the model.

BEISPIEL   einen Tag in München bleiben
          Er ist einen Tag in München geblieben.

1   2   3   4   5   6   7   8   9   10   11

VII. SYNTHESE

A. Was hat's im Fernsehen gegeben?   Hartmut is participating in a survey on television viewing. Listen as he describes last evening's fare. You will then hear five statements. Underline **richtig** if the

Copyright © 1989 by Holt, Rinehart and Winston, Inc. All rights reserved.

sentence is true and **falsch** if it is false. You will hear both the passage and the questions twice.

1. Hartmut hat bis spät in die Nacht ferngesehen. **richtig falsch**
2. Der Bericht über Japan hat 45 Minuten gedauert. **richtig falsch**
3. Der Krimi hat um neunzehn Uhr dreißig begonnen. **richtig falsch**
4. Hartmut hat den Dokumentarfilm nicht besonders interessant gefunden. **richtig falsch**
5. Heute abend sieht er wieder fern. **richtig falsch**

B. Persönliche Fragen. Answer the following five personal questions during the time provided. Each question will be asked twice.

1   2   3   4   5

Copyright © 1989 by Holt, Rinehart and Winston, Inc. All rights reserved.

PART TWO

I. BAUSTEIN 6.1: TELLING TIME; TIME EXPRESSIONS

A. Der Arbeitstag. Some employees are being interviewed about their daily routine. Using the following cues, tell how they answer.

Seldom on time!
*   At 20 minutes after 5.*
Around noon.
Between 8 and 9 o'clock.

From quarter after 2 to 2:30.
Actually eight hours.
Too early! At 7:15 a.m.

1. Wann beginnt der Tag für Sie?

_____

2. Wann trinken Sie Kaffee?

_____

3. Wann gehen Sie ins Büro?

_____

4. Wie lang dauert der Arbeitstag?

_____

5. Wann essen Sie zu Mittag?

_____

6. Und wann verlassen Sie das Büro?

_____

B. Eine Zugreise. An employee of the German Federal Railways in Essen is telling travelers when various trains run. Based on the schedule, how would the employee answer the following questions? Write out the time in full and convert 24-hour time to the 12-hour system.

Copyright © 1989 by Holt, Rinehart and Winston, Inc. All rights reserved.

BEISPIEL   Um wieviel Uhr gibt es am Abend einen Zug nach Duisburg?
Um sechs Uhr vierundzwanzig oder um zehn Minuten vor elf.

Von **Essen** nach

		Mainz	268 Tkm			Mannheim = M 343 Tkm Heidelberg = H 370 Tkm			
ab	Zug Nr	an	Bemerkungen	ab	Zug Nr	M an	H an	Bemerkungen
ⓖ✕4.52 E 638	8.02	Ⓤ Düsseldorf D 🍴		Ⓒ 4.52 E	638	9.37		Ⓤ Köln D 🍴
Ⓒ 6.23 🚅 111	8.58	🍴	6.23 🚅 111	9.42	9.54	✕
6.32 D 221	9.36		6.46 D 1513	10.45	10.58	✕
6.46 D 1513	9.57		6.52 D 211	10.59	11.12	✕
6.52 D 211	10.10	✕✕	7.08 D 503	11.05	11.41	Ⓤ Mannheim 2.
7.08 D 503	10.18	✕✕	7.54 🚅 113	11.13	11.25	✕
7.54 🚅 113	10.31	🍴	8.19 D 505	12.16	12.52	✕ Mannheim
8.19 D 505	11.26	✕	8.56 D 509	12.57		
8.56 D 509	12.12	✕✕	9.22 E 546	13.13	13.27	Ⓤ Duisburg D ✕
9.44 🚅 107	12.34	🍴	9.44 🚅 107	13.19	13.38	✕ Mannheim
10.07 D 1503	13.08		10.07 D 1503	13.53	14.20	Ⓤ Mannheim
10.18 E 2027	14.23		10.59 D 619		15.52	
10.59 D 619	14.23	✕ Ⓤ Koblenz E	Ⓐ 12.06 🚅 115	15.26	15.39	✕
Ⓐ 12.06 🚅 115	14.43		12.21 D 615	16.20	16.34	✕
12.21 D 615	15.29		Ⓐ 14.01 🚅 117	17.23	17.36	✕
12.57 E 346	16.27	Ⓤ Köln D ✕	14.20 D 517		18.30	
Ⓐ 14.01 🚅 117	16.39		14.20 D 517	18.47		Ⓤ Mainz
14.20 D 517	17.30	✕	15.05 🚅 167	18.28	18.40	✕
Ⓗ 15.05 🚅 167	17.44		15.59 🚅🚅 32	19.29	19.42	Ⓤ Köln
15.59 🚅🚅 32	18.45	Ⓤ Köln	16.12 D 523	20.56	21.14	Ⓤ Frankfurt E
16.12 D 523	19.07		Ⓑ 18.14 🚅🚅 34	21.35	21.48	✕
18.07 D 525	21.31	✕	18.24 E 2102	22.46	23.33	Ⓤ Duisburg D ✕ Mannheim
Ⓑ 18.14 🚅🚅 34	20.51		Ⓐ 20.05 🚅 132	0.50	1.10	Ⓤ Köln ✕
18.24 E 2102	21.36	Ⓤ Duisburg D ✕	Ⓕ 21.28 D 1315		2.03	Ⓤ Frankfurt E
19.03 E 2730	23.29	Ⓤ Köln D 🍴	Ⓕ 21.28 D 1315	2.13		Ⓤ Köln 🛏🛏
Ⓐ 20.05 🚅 132	22.48	Ⓤ Köln 🍴	22.28 D 209	2.56	3.23	🛏
21.18 D 625	0.45		22.50 D 227	3.00	3.23	Ⓤ Duisburg 🛏🛏 Mannheim
Ⓒ 21.28 D 1315	0.51		⊝23.02 D 611	3.53	4.16	🍴
22.28 D 209	1.52					
22.50 D 227	2.11	Ⓤ Duisburg	**Saarbrücken 360 Tkm**			
			Ⓐ 6.23 🚅 111	10.52		Ⓤ Koblenz 🛏E
Ⓐ Mo bis Fr			6.52 D 211	12.12		Ⓤ Köln 🍴
Ⓑ täglich außer Sa			8.19 D 505	14.02		Ⓤ Bingerbrück E
Ⓒ Mo bis Sa			Ⓔ 9.44 🚅 107	15.02		Ⓤ Koblenz E
Ⓓ Mo bis Fr, nicht 17. VI.			10.18 E 2027	16.20		Ⓤ Bingerbrück
Ⓔ nicht 27. IX.			10.59 D 619	16.20		Ⓤ Bingerbrück E
Ⓖ auch 17. VI.			Ⓐ 12.06 🚅 115	16.36		Ⓤ Koblenz 🛏E
Ⓗ Fr			12.32 E 2136	18.10		
			13.51 E 2029	19.50		🍴 Kaiserslautern Hbf D
⊝ ab Essen-Altenessen			15.27 D 603	20.24		
			Ⓐ 16.12 D 523	20.58		✕ Ⓤ Düsseldorf 🛏E 🍴
			17.37 D 344	22.43		✕ Ⓤ Köln D 🍴

1. Ein Zug kommt morgens um ein Uhr zweiundfünfzig in Mainz an, nicht wahr? Um wieviel Uhr verläßt er Essen?

   _____

2. Ich muß morgen nachmittag gegen halb drei in Mainz sein. Um wieviel Uhr geht ein Zug?

   _____

3. Es gibt einen Zug gegen acht Uhr abends. Um wieviel Uhr kommt er in Heidelberg an?

   _____

Copyright © 1989 by Holt, Rinehart and Winston, Inc. All rights reserved.   **106**

4. Ich möchte zwischen sieben und acht Uhr morgens nach Mannheim fahren. Um wieviel Uhr geht ein Zug?

_____

5. Um wieviel Uhr gibt es einen Zug nach Mannheim? Ich möchte am Samstag gegen Mittag fahren.

_____

6. Um neun Uhr achtundzwanzig fährt ein Zug nach Mainz, nicht wahr? Wann kommt man dort an?

_____

C. Unsere Familie. Herr Anker is telling when members of his family do certain things. Recreate his statements by combining elements from the following three columns below to form appropriate time expressions.

	am	Monat
	im	abends
	die	sonntags, montags, usw.
einmal, zweimal, usw.	heute	Woche
	morgen	Jahr
	jeden	früh
	jede	nachmittag (abend)
		Morgen (Nachmittag, Abend)

1. _____ gehe ich immer zur Bäckerei.

2. Wir kaufen _____ im Supermarkt ein, aber

_____ gehen wir zum Lebensmittelgeschäft.

3. _____ kauft meine Frau auf dem Markt ein.

4. _____ besuchen wir Oma Anker.

5. _____ machen wir Urlaub.

6. _____ gehen wir ins Theater, Kino oder

Konzert.

Copyright © 1989 by Holt, Rinehart and Winston, Inc. All rights reserved.

D. Und Sie? Combining elements from the columns above, write sentences about your activities. Use a different time expression for each.

1. _____

2. _____

3. _____

4. _____

5. _____

II. BAUSTEIN 6.2: PRESENT-PERFECT TENSE: IRREGULAR VERBS WITH <u>HABEN</u>

A. Am Wochenende. Complete Ingrid's diary notes with appropriate past participles of verbs from the list below.

BEISPIEL   Omas Koffer zum Bahnhof **getragen**

trinken	helfen	verlassen	sprechen
sehen	essen	liegen	
einladen	lesen	tragen	

1. Freitag abend: das Büro früher _____, einige Freunde

   zum Abendessen _____, dann einen Krimi im Fernse-

   hen _____

2. Samstag: am Morgen Vater im Garten _____, bei Inge

   zu Mittag _____, am Abend Johann

   _____, mit ihm eine Stunde über seine Reise

   _____

3. Sonntag: lange im Bett *(bed)* _____ und einen blöden

   Roman _____, am Nachmittag mit Arno und Luise

   Kaffee _____

Copyright © 1989 by Holt, Rinehart and Winston, Inc. All rights reserved.

B. Der Stromausfall. (Power outage.) The daily habits of many people were interrupted by a power outage. Recreate their statements telling how they and others altered their usual routine, by giving the present perfect of each of the following sentences.

BEISPIEL   Abends rufst du immer deinen Freund an.
            Aber gestern abend **hast du deinen Freund nicht angerufen.**

1. Nach dem Abendessen sieht Paula immer fern.

    Aber gestern abend _____.

2. Am Abend schreibe ich immer Briefe.

    Aber gestern abend _____.

3. Sie sitzen abends vor dem Fernseher.

    Aber gestern abend _____.

4. Um sieben Uhr beginnt ihr mit der Hausaufgabe.

    Aber gestern abend _____.

5. Ein romantischer Abend ohne Licht (light) gefällt mir.

    Aber gestern abend _____.

    _____.

III. BAUSTEIN 6.3: PRESENT-PERFECT TENSE: REGULAR VERBS WITH <u>HABEN</u>

A. Ein Nachmittag im Leben einer (of an) **amerikanischen Reisegruppe.**   The group leader for a foreign-study group has jotted down some notes about what members of her group did the first day in *Wien*. Translate her notes.

1. Kathy and Jeff changed money and bought sweaters in the clothing store near the train station.

    _____

    _____

Copyright © 1989 by Holt, Rinehart and Winston, Inc. All rights reserved.   **109**

2. Paul waited for two hours for his bus.

_____

3. Kate sent a package to her family in the U.S.

_____

_____

4. Lisa tried on a few dresses in a department store.

_____

_____

5. Allison brought along a map and showed her friends the city.

_____

_____

6. Amy took a trip to the Vienna Woods *(Wiener Wald)*.

_____

7. Julie and Jim played their guitars on the street corner and earned money.

_____

_____

8. I thought about my vacation in Switzerland!

_____

B. Und Sie? Using the model as a guide, indicate whether or not you have ever done the following things.

BEISPIEL   in einem Krankenhaus arbeiten
Ja, ich habe letzten Sommer in einem Krankenhaus gearbeitet.
or:

Copyright © 1989 by Holt, Rinehart and Winston, Inc. All rights reserved.   **110**

Nein, ich habe in keinem Krankenhaus gearbeitet, aber ich habe bei einem Tierarzt gearbeitet.

1. mit Billie Jean King Tennis spielen

    _____

    _____

2. Gold in Kalifornien suchen

    _____

    _____

3. in Beverly Hills einkaufen

    _____

    _____

4. einen Filmstar in Hollywood besuchen

    _____

    _____

5. einen Dokumentarfilm für das Fernsehen machen

    _____

    _____

6. in einem Luxushotel *(luxury hotel)* übernachten

    _____

    _____

IV. BAUSTEIN 6.4: PRESENT-PERFECT TENSE: VERBS WITH <u>SEIN</u>: PAST TENSE OF <u>SEIN</u>

A. In den Ferien. Margarete and Hans are talking about what they and others did last summer. Complete their conversation by filling in

Copyright © 1989 by Holt, Rinehart and Winston, Inc. All rights reserved.

the blanks with the present perfect of the verb in parentheses. Some verbs are conjugated with **sein,** others with **haben.**

1. Margarete: Wohin _____ du letzten Sommer

   _____ (reisen)?

2. Hans: Mein Bruder und ich _____ im Schwarzwald *(Black*

   Forest) _____ (wandern). Meine Schwester

   _____ nicht _____ (mitfahren), denn sie

   _____ in Salzburg in einem Hotel _____

   (arbeiten). Und du?

3. Margarete: Ich _____ nach Holland _____

   (fahren). Ich _____ einen Monat auf dem Land

   _____ (bleiben). Und im Juli _____ einige

   amerikanische Freunde zu Besuch *(for a visit)* _____

   (kommen).

4. Hans: Wie nett! Im August _____ meine Freunde Volker und

   Rolf in die Vereinigten Staaten _____ (fliegen). Sie

   _____ einige Probleme auf der Reise _____

   (haben). Ihr Flugzeug _____ zu spät in New York

   _____ (ankommen), und dann _____ sie ihre

   Koffer nicht _____ (finden). Dann _____ aber

   alles gut _____ (gehen). Sie _____ viele Leute

   _____ (kennenlernen) und _____ eigent-

   lich sehr glücklich _____ (zurückkommen).

Copyright © 1989 by Holt, Rinehart and Winston, Inc. All rights reserved.

B. Ein Krimi. In a TV detective story one of the characters uses the present tense to narrate firsthand a frightening experience. Put together the following clues and then retell her story using the present-perfect tense and the third person. Some of the verbs are conjugated with **sein,** others with **haben.**

BEISPIEL   Dann gehe ich zur Polizei.
Dann ist sie zur Polizei gegangen.

Sie sprechen ganz leise.
Ich rufe die Polizei an.
Es ist sehr dunkel.
Der Mann trägt einen langen,
   schwarzen Mantel.
Sie stehen vor der Tür.

Ein Mann und eine Frau
   gehen die Straße entlang.
Ich sitze vor dem Fenster.
Sie halten vor unserem Haus.
Ich finde die Situation sehr
   unangenehm.

_____

_____

_____

_____

_____

_____

_____

_____

_____

V. SYNTHESE

A. Unser Fernsehprogramm.   Imagine that you have been put in charge of a university television station. What programs would you include and what time would they be on the air? Describe five or more of the programs you would schedule.

Copyright © 1989 by Holt, Rinehart and Winston, Inc. All rights reserved.

BEISPIEL **Von neun bis zehn Uhr mogens gibt es Trickfilme auf deutsch für die Studenten in der Deutschstunde. Sie müssen kurz und interessant sein.**

_____

_____

_____

_____

_____

_____

_____

_____

_____

_____

B. Einige Stunden im Leben einer berühmten Person.

Imagine that you are a famous person (past or present) or create an imaginary celebrity. Using the following questions as a guide, describe several hours in the life of this person. Use a separate piece of paper for your paragraph.

Mit wem haben Sie gesprochen? Wohin sind Sie gegangen? Mit wem? Wo und wie viele Stunden haben Sie gearbeitet? Mit wem? Wo haben Sie zu Mittag/zu Abend gegessen?

Copyright © 1989 by Holt, Rinehart and Winston, Inc. All rights reserved.

KAPITEL 7 HEIM UND NACHBAR-SCHAFT

PART ONE

I. UND SIE?

A. Wo sind sie?   The Jägers have been house-hunting for several weeks, and have been through several houses. Listen to the following excerpts from their conversations, and decide which part of the house they are in. Write your answers in a German phrase in the spaces provided. You will hear each conversation twice.

BEISPIEL   Unser Sofa kann vor dem Fenster stehen, und in dieser Ecke der Sessel.

Beispiel **im Wohnzimmer**

1. _____   2. _____

3. _____   4. _____

5. _____   6. _____

B. Ganz im Gegenteil!   Karl and Karla's friends sometimes wonder why these two stay together. They just don't seem to see things the same way. Use opposites you have learned to tell how Karl responds to Karla's statements.

BEISPIEL   Karl! Findest du das Sofa bequem?
           Nein. Ich finde es unbequem.

1   2   3   4   5   6

Copyright © 1989 by Holt, Rinehart and Winston, Inc. All rights reserved.   **115**

II. AUSSPRACHE

Listen and then pronounce the following words.

A. Consonants

/ŋ/	Sendu**ng** Wohnu**ng** Werbu**ng** Kleidu**ng** la**ng**weilig la**ng**-sam e**ng** Vorha**ng**
/ng/	a**ng**enehm a**ng**ekommen a**ng**erufen
/ɪç/ — /ɪg/	wen**ig** — wen**ig**er langweil**ig** — langweil**ig**er bill**ig** — bill**ig**er wicht**ig** — wicht**ig**er schmutz**ig** — schmutz**ig**er ruh**ig** — ruh**ig**er

B. Vowels

/o/ — /φ/	gro**ß** — grö**ß**er h**o**ch — h**ö**her B**o**den — B**ö**den
/ɔ/ — /œ/	**o**ft — **ö**fter T**o**chter — T**ö**chter
/ɑ/ — /ɛ/	L**a**nd — l**ä**ndlich l**a**ng — l**ä**nger **a**lt — **ä**lter verl**a**ssen — verl**ä**ßt Vorh**a**ng — Vorh**ä**nge Schr**a**nk — Schr**ä**nke N**a**cht — N**ä**chte **A**pfel — **Ä**pfel
/ao/ — /ɔφ/	Tr**au**m — Tr**äu**me H**au**s — H**äu**ser l**au**fen — l**äu**ft B**au**m — B**äu**me
/u:/ — /y:/	F**u**ß — F**ü**ße
/U/ — /Y/	k**u**rz — k**ü**rzer j**u**ng — j**ü**nger m**u**ß — m**ü**ssen w**u**rden — w**ü**rden M**u**tter — M**ü**tter

C. Repeat the following sentences.

1. Deine Wohnung ist schmutzig, aber meine Wohnung ist schmutziger.
2. Beim Haus meiner Träume gibt's viele Bäume.
3. Ihre Töchter sind jünger als unsere Tochter.

III. BAUSTEIN 7.1: DEMONSTRATIVE PRONOUNS; <u>DER</u>-WORDS AS PRONOUNS

A. . . . und Funktion *(Vorteile und Nachteile.)*

B. Im Kaufhaus. The Biedermeiers are thinking of redecorating their house. Listen as they deliberate about some furnishings in a department store. Following each conversation, write in English the meaning of each demonstrative pronoun or **der**-word you hear in the spaces provided. You will hear each conversation twice.

Copyright © 1989 by Holt, Rinehart and Winston, Inc. All rights reserved. **116**

BEISPIEL   Gefallen dir diese Möbel?
          Nein, solche gefallen mir gar nicht.

Beispiel   <u>ones like that</u>

1. _____   2. _____

3. _____   4. _____

5. _____   6. _____

7. _____

*C. Beim Makler.   (At the agency.) The Wagners are in a real estate office looking at pictures of houses and apartments for rent. Give the real estate agent's answers to their questions.

BEISPIEL   Welches Haus hat drei Schlafzimmer? (dies-)
          Dieses hat drei Schlafzimmer.

1   2   3   4   5   6   7   8

IV. BAUSTEIN 7.2: COMPARATIVE AND SUPERLATIVE OF ADJECTIVES AND ADVERBS

A. . . . und Funktion *(Geht's ein wenig billiger?)*

B. Wir haben eine Wohnung für Sie!   Imagine you're assisting a real estate agent by studying current listings and making decisions about which properties to show. Read the listings, then listen to the housing needs of each client. Based on the information you read and hear, complete a report for each client by underlining the letter of the word or words that best complete the sentences. You will hear each client's needs twice.

Copyright © 1989 by Holt, Rinehart and Winston, Inc. All rights reserved.

BEISPIEL   Die Baers suchen ein neues Haus, aber es darf nicht zu teuer sein. Herr Baer verdient nur 2400 Mark im Monat.

Beispiel   Familie Baer: Haus Nr. 1 ist das Beste, weil es . . .
   a.   am billigsten ist.
   b.   am kleinsten ist.
   c.   am elegantesten ist.

1.   Ein Haus in der Stadt. Nähe Bahnhof. Klein, aber elegant. Moderne Küche und Bad; Sauna; Parkgarage.
40.000 DM

2.   6 Zi. historisches Landhaus im traditionellen Stil. Baujahr 1830. Viel Platz für Ihren Garten. 20 Min. von der Stadt.
100.000 DM

3.   In einer alten Gegend der Stadt. 8 Zi. Haus; Modern, neu renoviert. Nähe Kinderspielplatz u. Biergarten.
Nur 85.000 DM

1.   Familie Winkler: Haus Nr. 2 ist perfekt für sie, weil es . . .
   a. kleiner ist als Nr. 3.
   b. traditioneller ist als Nr. 1.
   c. ruhiger ist als Nr. 1 oder 3.
2.   Familie Maierhof: Für sie ist Haus Nr. 3 besonders gut. Es ist . . .
   a. näher zur Stadtmitte als Nr. 2.
   b. größer als Nr. 1 oder 2.
   c. moderner als Nr. 2.
3.   Die Architekturstudenten: Haus Nr. 2 ist richtig für sie, weil es . . .
   a. weiter von der Stadt ist als Haus Nr. 1.
   b. ruhiger ist als Haus Nr. 3.
   c. älter und traditioneller ist als Haus Nr. 3.

*C. Bei uns ist alles besser!   The Moellers are rather competitive and are constantly making rude comparisons. Follow the example to tell what they said at a neighborhood party.

BEISPIEL   Euer Sohn ist intelligent, . . .
   . . . aber unser Sohn ist viel intelligenter.

1   2   3   4   5   6

Copyright © 1989 by Holt, Rinehart and Winston, Inc. All rights reserved.   **118**

V. BAUSTEIN 7.3: GENITIVE CASE AND GENITIVE PREPOSITIONS

A. . . . und Funktion *(Auf dem Land.)*

B. So ein Fiasko!   Now that they are finally moving out, Gerd and Gerda are talking to a neighbor about the unhappy years they spent in their last apartment. Listen to what they say to various people and decide whether or not you hear a genitive construction each time. Check the column marked "yes" if you hear a genitive construction, and "no" if none is present. You will hear each item twice.

BEISPIEL   Während des Winters haben wir es hier zu kalt gefunden.

	YES	**NO**
Beispiel	✓	_____
1.	_____	_____
2.	_____	_____
3.	_____	_____
4.	_____	_____
5.	_____	_____
6.	_____	_____

C. Die Menschen und ihre Hunde.   The Hundewetters run a kennel, and each family member has his or her favorite pooch. You will hear several questions about the picture. Use the genitive case to answer each question in the spaces provided. You will hear each question twice.

Copyright © 1989 by Holt, Rinehart and Winston, Inc. All rights reserved.

BEISPIEL Hinter wessen Hund steht ein Hundehaus?
Hinter dem Hund des Vaters.

der Vater

die Mutter

die Tochter

der Sohn

1. _____

2. _____

3. _____

4. _____

5. _____

6. _____

Copyright © 1989 by Holt, Rinehart and Winston, Inc. All rights reserved. **120**

VI. BAUSTEIN 7.4: SIMPLE PAST OF MODAL VERBS

A. ... und Funktion *(Der Umzug.)*

B. Feuer! Listen as people talk about their experiences when the Pech family's apartment is gutted by fire while the Pechs are on vacation. After each neighbor speaks, underline the letter of the phrase that best answers the question. You will hear each person speak twice.

1. Why did the Biedermanns wait in the parking lot?
   a. they wanted to   b. they were supposed to   c. they had to
2. Why didn't Hänschen watch the fire from the balcony?
   a. he didn't want to   b. he wasn't able to   c. he wasn't permitted to
3. Why didn't the neighbors save all the furniture?
   a. they weren't permitted to   b. they weren't able to   c. they didn't want to
4. Why did Frau Edel call the Pech family?
   a. she wanted to   b. she was supposed to   c. she had to

*C. Nicht wie früher. Horst and Helga are talking about some changes that have occurred over the past ten years. Each time that Horst mentions something in the present, it reminds Helga of the past. Using the cues, give Horst's comments.

BEISPIEL   Heute wollen viele Studenten ein Fahrrad kaufen. (früher ein Auto)
   Früher wollten viele Studenten ein Auto kaufen.

1   2   3   4   5   6   7   8

VII. SYNTHESE

A. Schönlage. Listen as Max Weber, a famous city planner, talks about *Schönlage,* the model town that he created. You will then hear six statements. Given the type of description Max Weber gave of his master plan, decide whether he is likely to have made these statements in a subsequent interview with reporters. Underline **ja** if he might have made the statement or **nein** if he would not have made the statement. Both the passage and the statements will be read twice.

Copyright © 1989 by Holt, Rinehart and Winston, Inc. All rights reserved.   **121**

1. ja nein   2. ja nein
3. ja nein   4. ja nein
5. ja nein   6. ja nein

B. Und Sie? A German-speaking person is asking you about what your ideal town looks like. Answer the questions in the pauses provided. Each question will be asked twice.

1   2   3   4

Copyright © 1989 by Holt, Rinehart and Winston, Inc. All rights reserved.

PART TWO

I. BAUSTEIN 7.1: DEMONSTRATIVE PRONOUNS; <u>DER</u>-WORDS AS PRONOUNS

A. Fragen, Fragen. There are many questions to ask when looking for a place to live. Complete the sentences with the appropriate **der**-word as pronoun.

BEISPIEL   Die Küche hier, hat ___**die**___ einen Küchenschrank?

1. Das Zimmer in der Zeitung, ist _____ noch frei?

2. Die Villa auf dem Berg, ist _____ sehr teuer?

3. Die Wohnung in der Auerstraße, wie viele Zimmer hat _____ denn?

4. Dieser Schrank hier, ist _____ neu?

5. Und das Badezimmer, ist _____ nicht sehr altmodisch?

6. Zwei Arbeitszimmer, aber sind _____ nicht zu dunkel?

B. Auf der Wohnungssuche. Erwin is looking at various neighbor-hoods and apartments with Frau Hammer, a real estate agent. Complete their statements by providing the appropriate form of the demonstrative pronoun indicated or the **der**-word used as a pronoun.

1. Frau Hammer: Die Geschäfte in dieser Straße sind sehr elegant.

    _____ (Everyone) will hier wohnen.

    Erwin: Ich aber nicht. In _____ (ones such as those) kaufe

    ich nie ein!

2. Frau Hammer: Diese Wohnung ist teuer, aber sehr schick.

    Erwin: In _____ (that one) gefällt mir aber der Teppich-

    boden nicht.

Copyright © 1989 by Holt, Rinehart and Winston, Inc. All rights reserved.   **123**

3. Frau Hammer: In dieser Nachbarschaft gibt es einige gute Lebens-

   mittelgeschäfte.

   Erwin: Ja, aber _____ *(all of them)* machen zu Mittag zu,

   nicht wahr?

4. Frau Hammer: _____ *(This one)* hier ist eine Wohnung für

   Sie. In _____ *(that one)* haben Sie alles.

   Erwin: _____ *(Which one)* meinen Sie?

   _____ *(The one)* mit dem Balkon?

5. Frau Hammer: Gefallen Ihnen die Zimmer? _____ *(Some of*

   them) sind ziemlich dunkel.

   Erwin: Ja, _____ *(that)* ist wahr. Aber die Terrasse!

   _____ *(It)* gefällt mir.

6. Frau Hammer: An der Ecke ist eine Haltestelle. Sie können mit der

   Straßenbahn in die Stadt fahren.

   Erwin: Aber nicht _____ *(every one)* hält hier, oder?

II. BAUSTEIN 7.2: COMPARATIVE AND SUPERLATIVE OF ADJECTIVES AND ADVERBS

A. Vor- und Nachteile.   The Mölter family is thinking of moving. Now that they have found a house they might like, they list the advantages and disadvantages to help them decide. Complete Frau Mölter's statements by choosing from the following adjectives and adverbs. Use each word only once and in the comparative form.

VORTEILE: modern, nah, jung, hell, bequem, gemütlich, gut, groß, oft

1. Der Garten ist _____ als unser Garten zu Hause.

Copyright © 1989 by Holt, Rinehart and Winston, Inc. All rights reserved.

2. Das Wohnzimmer ist _____ und

   _____ .

3. Die Küche ist _____ und _____ .

4. Die Lage *(location)* ist _____ für mich. Das Haus ist

   _____ zur Uni.

5. Die Nachbarn sind _____ . Monika kann

   _____ mit den Kindern in der Nachbarschaft spielen

   als in unserer Gegend.

NACHTEILE: klein, teuer, hoch, viel, gern, unpraktisch, dunkel, laut, alt

1. Die Miete ist _____ .

2. Die Schlafzimmer sind _____ und die Schränke sind

   _____ .

3. Das Arbeitszimmer ist _____ .

4. Das Haus ist _____ und es gibt viele Reparaturen

   (repairs) zu machen.

5. Wir müssen neue Möbel kaufen; das wird _____ als ich

   gedacht habe.

6. Die Straße ist _____ , denn es gibt _____

   Geschäfte und Autos.

7. Wir haben unser altes Haus _____ !

Copyright © 1989 by Holt, Rinehart and Winston, Inc. All rights reserved.   **125**

das billigste Benzin der Region

Liter –.96 SUPER BP FORMEL CE

Grossmarkt JUMBO Villars-sur-Glâne

B. Meinungen über München. Susan will soon visit *München* and has asked a German acquaintance his opinion on various aspects of the city. Using the cues provided and following the model, recreate her friend's answers to her questions.

BEISPIEL Welches Restaurant finden Sie besonders gut? (die Gaststätte Leopold)
Die Gaststätte Leopold ist am besten.

1. Welches Museum ist besonders interessant? (das Deutsche Museum)

   _____

2. Welches Hotel in der Stadtmitte ist gemütlich? (das Hotel Beck)

   _____

3. Welche Bierhalle besuchen die Touristen oft? (das Hofbräuhaus)

   _____

Copyright © 1989 by Holt, Rinehart and Winston, Inc. All rights reserved. **126**

4. In welche Bierhalle gehen die Münchner gern? (die Augustiner Bierhalle)

_____

5. Welchen Park finden Sie besonders schön? (der Englische Garten)

_____

6. Welche Gegend finden Sie besonders interessant? (Schwabing)

_____

III. BAUSTEIN 7.3: GENITIVE CASE AND GENITIVE PREPOSITIONS

A. Das gefällt mir nicht.   Michael is looking for an apartment and seems very hard to please. Using the cues provided and following the model, recreate his statements and questions to the landlady.

BEISPIEL   die Balkons/diese Wohnungen/sein/zu klein
Die Balkons dieser Wohnungen sind zu klein.

1. Die Farbe/dieser Teppichboden/sein/absolut geschmacklos

_____

2. sein/es/hier/auch/während/der Tag/ruhig/?

_____

3. durch/die Fenster/dieses Zimmer/sehen/man/nur/der Parkplatz

_____

4. stehen/das Auto/der Nachbar/immer/vor/die Tür/?

_____

5. was/sein/die Vorteile/diese Wohnung/?

_____

6. trotz/der Garten/gefallen/ich/die Wohnung/nicht

_____

Copyright © 1989 by Holt, Rinehart and Winston, Inc. All rights reserved.

B. Fragen, Fragen. Uschi is asking her friend Peter a lot of questions. Using the cues provided and following the model, supply Peter's answers.

BEISPIEL   Was findest du schwer? *(the life of a student)*
   Ich finde das Leben eines Studenten schwer.

1. Was ist Frau Engelmann von Beruf? *(director of a company)*

   _____

2. Wann kaufst du ein Auto? *(one day)*

   _____

3. Wer ist Frau Schwarz? *(my father's sister)*

   _____

4. Warum spielst du heute nicht Tennis? *(because of the weather)*

   _____

5. Wessen Adresse ist das? *(Sabine's)*

   _____

6. Wann gehst du nicht aus? *(during the week)*

   _____

C. Sehen, kaufen, einziehen.   Use the guidelines below to create an ad for some most unusual living quarters.

BEISPIEL   Sind Sie unglücklich über **den Preis der Häuser?**
   der Preis/die Häuser

1. Wo Sie jetzt wohnen: sind Sie unglücklich über

   _____ _____?
   die Kosten/die Miete
   der Hund/die Nachbarn
   ?

Copyright © 1989 by Holt, Rinehart and Winston, Inc. All rights reserved.   **128**

2. Dann sehen Sie _____ _____ !

    das Haus/Ihre Träume
    der Vorteil/diese Gegend
    ?

3. Sie sind allein auf dem Land in der Nähe _____ .

    die Wüste *(wilderness)*
    ein Zoo
    ?

4. Statt _____ haben Sie einen Wasserfall; statt

    das Badezimmer
    ein Schwimmbecken
    ?

    _____ hören Sie die Geräusche *(sounds)*

    der Fernseher
    das Telefon
    ?

    _____ .

    der Wald
    das Dschungel *(jungle)*
    ?

5. Während _____ ist es sehr warm; während

    der Sommer
    der Abend
    ?

    _____ ist es angenehm kalt.

    der Winter
    der Abend
    ?

6. Preis: nur 1000 DM!

Copyright © 1989 by Holt, Rinehart and Winston, Inc. All rights reserved. **129**

IV. BAUSTEIN 7.4: SIMPLE PAST OF MODAL VERBS

A. Vorteile und Nachteile.   Herr and Frau Stobel have different perspectives when they reflect on an apartment they lived in for several years. Complete their conversation by filling in the blanks with the simple past forms of the modal verbs **dürfen, können, müssen, sollen,** and **wollen.**

HERR STOBEL: Die Wohnung in der Auerstraße hat mir gut gefallen,

denn wir _____ nicht viel Miete bezahlen. Die Kinder

_____ im Garten spielen, und wir _____ auch

Haustiere haben. Anneliese _____ zu Fuß zur Schule gehen,

und du _____ in unserem Arbeitszimmer ruhig arbeiten. Ich

_____ länger in der Wohnung bleiben, aber wir

_____ wegen deines Berufs umziehen.

FRAU STOBEL: Ich habe nicht alles so schön und idyllisch gefunden!

Du _____ in dieser ruhigen Nachbarschaft am Wald wohnen,

aber wir _____ täglich 40 Minuten in die Stadt fahren. Du

_____ die Straßenbahn nehmen, und ich _____

mit dem Auto fahren, aber dann _____ du oft früher im Büro

sein und hast das Auto gebraucht. Ich _____ dann ohne Auto

sein. Und wir _____ viele Leute kennenlernen, aber wir haben

keinen Kontakt mit unseren Nachbarn gehabt. Nein, ich _____

nie sagen, daß das die Wohnung meiner Träume war.

B. Meine Familie.   Complete the following sentences in the simple past to describe an actual or imagined activity in your or your family's past.

Copyright © 1989 by Holt, Rinehart and Winston, Inc. All rights reserved.   **130**

1. (wollen) Ich _____

2. (müssen) Meine Familie _____

3. (mögen) Meine Mutter _____

4. (dürfen) Ich _____

5. (sollen) Mein Vater _____

6. (können) Ich _____

V. SYNTHESE

A. Heim und Nachbarschaft.   Using the information given in the
Synthese and **Land und Leute** readings as a point of departure,
write a brief description of your ideal neighborhood and/or town.

_____

_____

_____

_____

_____

_____

_____

_____

_____

_____

_____

_____

_____

Copyright © 1989 by Holt, Rinehart and Winston, Inc. All rights reserved.

B. Wohnstil. The following six drawings represent some of the popular basic decors in the Bundesrepublik. Choose one that you find most attractive or choose items of furniture from various rooms to create the living room you would like to have. Using the questions as a guide, write a paragraph in which you describe the reasons for your choice and make comparisons with some other room styles. Use a separate sheet of paper.

Copyright © 1989 by Holt, Rinehart and Winston, Inc. All rights reserved.

1. Welche Möbelstücke gefallen Ihnen am besten?
2. Welchen Stil finden Sie am geschmackvollsten, bequemsten, schicksten, usw.?
3. Welches Zimmer ist altmodischer, (un)gemütlicher, (un)moderner, dunkler, usw. als _____?

Copyright © 1989 by Holt, Rinehart and Winston, Inc. All rights reserved.   **133**

KAPITEL 8 GESUND SEIN, FIT SEIN

PART ONE

I. UND SIE?

A. Fitness-Tips.   Gertrud, Arnold, and Klaus are guests on a television fitness show. They are telling about their health regimens. Record their activities and habits by writing the name of the activities or habits under the correct column. You will hear each speaker twice.

BEISPIEL   Ich trinke nie Alkohol—das ist am wichtigsten. Ich schwimme täglich und mache dreimal die Woche Fitnesstraining.

	DAILY	2–4 TIMES/ WEEK	WEEKLY	NOW AND THEN	NEVER
Beispiel	swim	fitness training	_____	_____	alcohol
1. Gertrud					
	_____	_____	_____	_____	_____
2. Arnold					
	_____	_____	_____	_____	_____
3. Klaus					
	_____	_____	_____	_____	_____

Copyright © 1989 by Holt, Rinehart and Winston, Inc. All rights reserved.

B. Was fehlt ihnen? (What's wrong with them?) Listen to the following people describe their physical complaints. On the figures, circle for each speaker the parts of the body affected. You will hear each description twice.

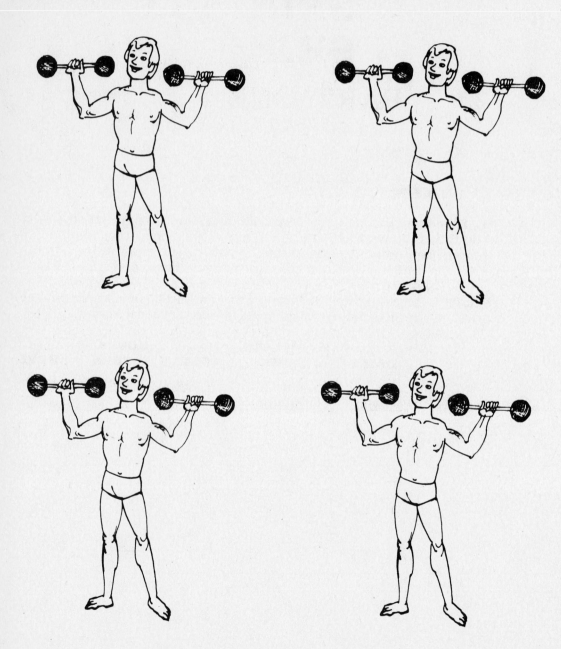

Copyright © 1989 by Holt, Rinehart and Winston, Inc. All rights reserved.

II. BAUSTEIN 8.1: REFLEXIVE CONSTRUCTIONS; REFLEXIVE PRONOUNS IN THE ACCUSATIVE CASE

A. . . . und Funktion *(Was fehlt Ihnen denn?)*

Gesundheit ist…

Spaß am Sport mit guter Kondition

trimm   SPORT-BILLY

B. Im Sportverein. The following comments were heard at an athletic club in Austria. For each comment you hear, determine whether or not a reflexive construction is present. Put a check mark in the appropriate column. You will hear each comment twice.

BEISPIEL   Sie müssen sich aber entspannen, Rolf!

	REFLEXIVE	NOT REFLEXIVE
Beispiel	✓	_____
1.	_____	_____
2.	_____	_____
3.	_____	_____
4.	_____	_____
5.	_____	_____
6.	_____	_____

Copyright © 1989 by Holt, Rinehart and Winston, Inc. All rights reserved.

*C. Beim Arzt.　Helmut is at the clinic for his annual checkup. Using the cues, give Helmut's answers to his doctor's questions.

BEISPIEL　Wie oft können Sie sich entspannen?　(eigentlich nie)
Ich kann mich eigentlich nie entspannen.

1　　2　　3　　4　　5　　6　　7　　8

III.　BAUSTEIN 8.2: REFLEXIVES WITH THE DATIVE; DATIVE WITH PARTS OF THE BODY

A.　. . . und Funktion (Routine.)

B. In der Sport-Boutique.　The following comments were heard at a sale in a sports boutique. For each reflexive construction you hear, determine whether the pronoun is in the dative or the accusative case. Put a check mark in the appropriate column. You will hear each comment twice.

BEISPIEL　Zieh dir diese Ski-Hose an, Margaret!

	DATIVE	ACCUSATIVE
Beispiel	✓	
1.		
2.		

Copyright © 1989 by Holt, Rinehart and Winston, Inc. All rights reserved.

3. _____ _____

4. _____ _____

5. _____ _____

6. _____ _____

*C. Morgenroutine.   Use the cues to say what Frau Gerhardt tells her children in order to get them off to school in time.

BEISPIEL   Hannes: sich die Ohren waschen
Hannes, wasch dir die Ohren!

1   2   3   4   5   6

IV.   BAUSTEIN 8.3: ADJECTIVE ENDINGS; ADJECTIVES AFTER DER-WORDS

A. . . . und Funktion *(In meiner Freizeit . . .)*

B. Im Klub.   The Hofnagels work in a health spa. Listen as they talk about various things. For each statement indicate what case the adjective construction is in. You will hear each statement twice.

BEISPIEL   Nach einem schweren Essen soll man nicht schwimmen, Herr Dicker!

	NOMINATIVE	ACCUSATIVE	DATIVE	GENITIVE
Beispiel	_____	_____	✔ _____	_____
1.	_____	_____	_____	_____
2.	_____	_____	_____	_____
3.	_____	_____	_____	_____
4.	_____	_____	_____	_____
5.	_____	_____	_____	_____
6.	_____	_____	_____	_____

Copyright © 1989 by Holt, Rinehart and Winston, Inc. All rights reserved.

C. Fragen, Fragen. Irene has allowed her son Alfred to accompany her as she cleans the sports club. Use the cues to tell how she answers his questions.

BEISPIEL   In welchem Zimmer soll ich auf dich warten? (klein, weiß)
In dem kleinen weißen Zimmer.

1   2   3   4   5   6

V.   BAUSTEIN 8.4: <u>DA</u>- AND <u>WO</u>-COMPOUNDS

A. . . . und Funktion *(Gesundheitstest.)*

B. Konversationen. You will hear four short conversations, each repeated twice. Answer the questions by circling the letter of the word or words that best complete the sentence.

1. In this conversation the word *daran* refers to:
    a. the bathing suit   b. the postcards   c. the water
2. In this conversation the word *darüber* refers to:
    a. politics   b. university policy   c. a professor's indiscretion
3. In this conversation the word *dagegen* refers to:
    a. the Berlin team   b. sports   c. high salaries for athletes
4. In this conversation the word *daran* refers to:
    a. people's jobs   b. stress at work   c. health

*C. Bei dem Deutschen Turn- und Sportbund.   Elke works at a DTSB office in Leipzig. She and a colleague are getting organized for the day's work. Use the cues to give Elke's answers to her colleague's questions.

BEISPIEL   Haben Sie Frau Fischer für die Information gedankt? (ja, schon)
Ja, ich habe ihr schon dafür gedankt.

Sprechen Sie heute mit Herrn Vogel? (nein, heute nicht)
Nein, ich spreche heute nicht mit ihm.

1   2   3   4   5   6   7   8

VI.   SYNTHESE

A. Lieblingssport.   Listen as Margarete and Alfred discuss the sports they enjoy. You will then hear five questions. In the spaces provided,

Copyright © 1989 by Holt, Rinehart and Winston, Inc. All rights reserved.

write the answers to these questions in German, using complete sentences. Both the passage and the questions will be read twice.

1. Was ist Margaretes Lieblingssport?

   _____

2. Wie findet Alfred das Skilaufen?

   _____

3. Wie oft hat Alfred das Skilaufen probiert?

   _____

4. Welchen Sport hat Alfred besonders gern, und welchen treibt er nur manchmal?

   _____

   _____

5. Was weiß Margarete über das Laufen?

   _____

B. Und Sie? Imagine that a German-speaking friend has asked you what your favorite sport is, either as participant or observer. You may write down a few notes in German, then begin speaking when you hear the tone. Include the following points:

—the name of your favorite sport
—why you like it
—where you do or see this sport
—whether it is for a particular season only

Notizen (notes):_____

_____

_____

_____

_____

Copyright © 1989 by Holt, Rinehart and Winston, Inc. All rights reserved.

PART TWO

I. BAUSTEIN 8.1: REFLEXIVE CONSTRUCTIONS; REFLEXIVE PRONOUNS IN THE ACCUSATIVE CASE

A. Im Sportverein.   Herr Schwarzenegger, a physical fitness consultant, has given the following advice to help his clients stay in good shape. Using the cues provided and following the model, recreate his statements. Use the appropriate form, familiar or polite.

BEISPIEL   Herr Wimpf, __beeilen Sie sich__ nicht so sehr! (sich beeilen)

1. Herr Friedl, _____ am Wochenende! (sich

   entspannen)

2. Johann und Inge, ihr _____ mehr Gymnastik und

   weniger Pizza _____! (müssen/sich gewöhnen an)

3. Elke, nach unserem Programm _____

   sicher wieder fit. (sich fühlen)

4. Frau Meyer, warum _____ nicht

   _____ Gymnastik? (sich interessieren für)

5. Meine Damen und Herren, _____ nicht,

   daß ich Ihnen keine Komplimente mache! (sich ärgern)

Copyright © 1989 by Holt, Rinehart and Winston, Inc. All rights reserved.

FITNESSCENTER NEUBAU

7, STIFTGASSE 27 ● TEL. 93 94 04

● BODYBUILDING FÜR DAMEN UND HERREN
● SAUNA, SOLARIUM, MASSAGE
● AEROBIC
● KONDITIONSTRAINING
● CELLULITISTRAINING
● GEZIELTE FIGURKORREKTUR DURCH HANTELTRAINING

DAS HOLT DIE OMA AUS DEM KOMA!

B. Meine Kondition?   Imagine that you have applied for membership in an elite health club and have been asked to write a paragraph about your physical condition, including your health habits, athletic interests, and lifestyle. Exaggerate, if you wish, in order to impress the screening committee. Write your paragraph on a separate sheet of paper.

II. BAUSTEIN 8.2: REFLEXIVES WITH THE DATIVE; DATIVE WITH PARTS OF THE BODY

A. Aktivitäten.   Choose from the following reflexive verbs and phrases to make comments about or give advice to the people listed below.

sich ärgern über ____?____   sich rasieren
sich ____?____ kaufen   sich freuen über ____?____
sich interessieren für ____?____   sich entspannen
sich ____?____ ansehen   sich gewöhnen an ____?____
sich ____?____ waschen   sich die Zähne putzen
sich freuen auf ____?____

BEISPIEL   Ich **soll mich mehr für Sport interessieren.**

1.   Die Studenten hier _____.

2.   Du sollst _____.

3.   Wir _____.

Copyright © 1989 by Holt, Rinehart and Winston, Inc. All rights reserved.

4. Der (Die) Präsident(in) von unserer Uni _____

_____ .

5. Ich _____ .

6. Unser(e) Deutschprofessor(in) _____

_____ .

7. ? _____ .

B. Der Egoist. Using the reflexive verbs that follow, complete the paragraph in which Hugo Selbstlob, a real egotist, talks about himself. The reflexives may be with either the accusative or the dative.

VERBEN: sich ansehen, sich fühlen, sich duschen, sich ärgern, sich rasieren, sich gewöhnen, sich interessieren, sich beeilen, sich kämmen, sich anziehen, sich entspannen

Meine Gesundheit. Ich kann sagen, daß ich _____ immer wohl

_____ . Ich _____ _____ nie, denn

Streß und Hektik sind nicht gut für meine Gesundheit. Ich treibe täglich

Sport und _____ _____ dann in der Sauna.

Meine Interessen. Ich _____ _____ für alles und

sage immer, was ich denke. Ich habe viele Freunde, denn alle Menschen

finden mich toll. Ich bin sehr flexibel und _____ _____

schnell an neue Leute und Situationen. Ich _____

_____ aber sehr über Menschen, die *(who)* nicht so intelligent und aktiv

sind wie ich.

Mein Alltag. Mein Tag beginnt um 6 Uhr 30. Zuerst *(First of all)*

_____ ich _____ . Dann _____ ich

Copyright © 1989 by Holt, Rinehart and Winston, Inc. All rights reserved. **145**

_____. Dann _____ ich _____ die Haare. Dann

_____ ich _____ einen neuen Trainingsanzug _____

Ich _____ _____ im Spiegel _____ und verstehe,

warum alle Menschen mir so viele Komplimente machen.

III. BAUSTEIN 8.3: ADJECTIVE ENDINGS; ADJECTIVES AFTER DER-WORDS

A. Ja, das meine ich auch. Werner thinks he can be a good friend just by agreeing completely with others when they talk about sports. Complete his statements with the appropriate endings on the **der-**words and adjectives.

1. Ich gehe auch nicht gern zu dies_____ alt_____, schmutzig_____

   Schwimmbad.

2. Dies_____ gefährlich_____ Sport treibe ich auch nie.

3. Ich kaufe solch_____ unbequem_____ Sportschuhe auch nicht.

4. Ich spiele auch nicht gern gegen d_____ aggressiv_____ Sportler.

5. D_____ meist_____ Sportvereine sind mir auch zu teuer.

6. Nach dies_____ schwer_____ Fitnessprogramm fühle ich mich auch

   ziemlich schwach.

7. Ich interessiere mich auch nicht für solch_____ blöd_____ Gesund-

   heitstests.

8. Ich sehe mir auch nicht gern dies_____ langweilig_____ Sportsendungen

   an.

B. Nach der Arbeit. The following comments were overheard in a **Kneipe,** where a group of coworkers are relaxing after work. Recreate their comments by filling in the blanks with the appropriate form of the **der-**word and the adjective in parentheses.

Copyright © 1989 by Holt, Rinehart and Winston, Inc. All rights reserved.   **146**

1. Ich ärgere mich über _____ _____ (those

   boring) Sendungen im Fernsehen. Ich habe mir _____

   _____ (the most expensive) Fernseher gekauft, aber

   _____ _____ (which intelligent) Mensch will

   sich _____ _____ (the stupid) Abendsendun-

   gen ansehen? Ich nicht!

2. Ich kann mich einfach nicht an _____ _____

   (the cold) Wetter gewöhnen. Ich bin Mitglied _____

   _____ (of the new) Sportvereins, aber wie soll man bei

   _____ _____ (this bad) Wetter Sport treiben?

3. Ich kann _____ _____ (the young) Leute von

   heute nicht verstehen. Sie tragen _____ _____

   (the most tasteless) Kleider. Sie interessieren sich nur für _____

   _____ (this terrible) Musik und sitzen immer nur in

   _____ _____ (the dark) Kneipen.

4. Moment mal! Wir treffen uns hier nach _____

   _____ (the long) Arbeitstag, weil wir uns entspannen

   wollen! Warum sprecht ihr nur über _____

   _____ (such unpleasant) Dinge (things)? Und ihr habt

   gar nicht recht. Nicht alle Fernsehsendungen sind langweilig und blöd.

   Ich finde zum Beispiel _____ _____ (the

   many) Dokumentarfilme sehr gut. Und Franz, du kannst in

Copyright © 1989 by Holt, Rinehart and Winston, Inc. All rights reserved.

_____ _____ _____ (the

beautiful, new) Sporthalle (fem.) Gymnastik treiben. Und nicht

_____ _____ (all young) Menschen sind so,

wie du sagst, Elfriede! _____ _____

_____ (Most young) Leute sind nicht anders als wir.

Übrigens fühle ich mich in _____ _____ (this

dark) Kneipe sehr wohl!

IV. BAUSTEIN 8.4: DA- AND WO-COMPOUNDS

A. Ein Supersportler. As a soccer super star, Rudi Tor has at-
tracted a lot of attention from the media. In this radio interview Rudi
is asked a wide range of questions. Using the cues, give Rudi's answers
to the questions.

BEISPIEL   Gewöhnen sich die Leute an die neuen Trimm-dich-Pfade? (ja,
langsam)
Ja, sie gewöhnen sich langsam daran.

Sprechen Sie mit Ihrer Familie über Sport? (nur ab und zu)
Ich spreche mit ihr nur ab und zu darüber.

1.   Haben Sie Zeit für ein Interview? (ja)

_____

2.   Können Sie sich vor einem Spiel entspannen? (ja, ein wenig)

_____

3.   Freuen Sie sich über die enthusiastischen Zuschauer (spectators)? (ja,
sehr)

_____

4.   Freuen Sie sich auf das nächste Spiel? (nein, eigentlich nicht)

_____

Copyright © 1989 by Holt, Rinehart and Winston, Inc. All rights reserved.

5. Interessieren sich die meisten Sportler für die Gesundheitsprobleme unserer Nation? (nein, leider nicht)

_____

_____

6. Sprechen Sie mit Ihren Fans über die Trimm-dich-Bewegung (movement)? (ja, so oft wie möglich)

_____

_____

B. Und Sie? Imagine you are a reporter interviewing a famous athlete. Using **wo-** compounds, write four questions you might want to ask him or her.

BEISPIEL **Wofür interessieren Sie sich außer Sport?**

1. _____

2. _____

3. _____

4. _____

V. SYNTHESE

A. Das Fahrrad. Refer to the **Synthese** reading **Trendsetter fahren Velo** in your textbook. In your opinion, what are the potential benefits and disadvantages in the development of bicycles as a major means of transportation in American cities?

Vorteile des Fahrrads:

_____

_____

_____

_____

Copyright © 1989 by Holt, Rinehart and Winston, Inc. All rights reserved.

Nachteile des Fahrrads:

_____

_____

_____

_____

B. Bei der Ärztin.   Refer to the drawing below and imagine the three-way dialogue that might take place between the doctor, patient, and nurse. It may be serious or amusing. Use a separate piece of paper to write the exchange, and include the following vocabulary:

Fieber   Schmerzen   weh tun   Bauch   Was fehlt . . . ?

Copyright © 1989 by Holt, Rinehart and Winston, Inc. All rights reserved.

KAPITEL **9 MAHLZEIT!**

PART ONE

I. UND SIE?

Im Restaurant.   Imagine that you work as a waiter or waitress in a German restaurant in the Midwest. The cook is in a panic because a busload of German tourists has just arrived, and no one in the kitchen speaks German. Of course, you will save the day. Your customers will place their orders only once, however, so be sure to take notes in German while they speak. After each of the four guests has ordered, translate the orders for the kitchen.

1. *Notizen (notes):* _____

_____

2. *Notizen:* _____

_____

3. *Notizen:* _____

_____

4. *Notizen:* _____

_____

Now compile and translate your order for the kitchen:

Copyright © 1989 by Holt, Rinehart and Winston, Inc. All rights reserved.

II. BAUSTEIN 9.1: <u>LIEGEN/(SICH) LEGEN;</u> <u>SITZEN/(SICH) SETZEN; STEHEN/STELLEN</u>

A. . . . und Funktion *(Den Tisch decken.)*

B. Im Hotel. Hanni is helping to set up and serve a large banquet at a hotel. Listen to some of the things she hears, and for each sentence, decide whether motion or location is being expressed. Put a check mark in the appropriate column. You will hear each sentence twice.

BEISPIEL   Soll ich das Fleisch zwischen das Gemüse und die Salate stellen?

	MOTION	LOCATION
Beispiel	✓	
1.		

Copyright © 1989 by Holt, Rinehart and Winston, Inc. All rights reserved.   **152**

2.   _____ _____

3.   _____ _____

4.   _____ _____

5.   _____ _____

6.   _____ _____

*C. Haben Sie's gemacht? Hugo, an apprentice waiter, is learning how to set a table and wait on customers. The headwaiter asks if Hugo has completed everything correctly. Hugo says that he has. Give his answers, according to the **Beispiel.**

BEISPIEL   Haben Sie die Tassen neben die Teller gestellt?
        Ja, die Tassen stehen neben den Tellern.

        Haben Sie die Löffel neben die Messer gelegt?
        Ja, die Löffel liegen neben den Messern.

1   2   3   4   5   6

III. BAUSTEIN 9.2: ADJECTIVES AFTER EIN-WORDS

A. . . . und Funktion *(Ist hier noch frei?)*

B. Warum ist Udo Punk so beliebt? Udo Punk, a famous rock star, is the topic of discussion on a call-in radio program. Listen to what various callers have to say about his popularity. Then for each sentence you hear, decide which case the **ein**-word and attributive adjectives are in. Put a check mark in the corresponding column. You will hear each comment twice.

BEISPIEL   Ich bin ein großer Fan von Udo Punk.

	NOMINATIVE	ACCUSATIVE	DATIVE	GENITIVE
Beispiel	✓			
1.				
2.				

Copyright © 1989 by Holt, Rinehart and Winston, Inc. All rights reserved.   **153**

3. _____ _____ _____

4. _____ _____ _____

5. _____ _____ _____

6. _____ _____ _____

*C. Das möchten wir nicht. In the "**Gasthaus zur Sonne**" Hartmut finds many dishes that sound appealing, but his friends don't want to order any of them. Give their answers to his suggestions.

BEISPIEL   Die hausgemachte Wurst schmeckt gut.
           Ja, aber wir möchten keine hausgemachte Wurst.

1   2   3   4   5   6   7   8

IV.   BAUSTEIN 9.3: UNPRECEDED ATTRIBUTIVE ADJECTIVES

A.   . . . und Funktion *(Keinen Appetit auf . . .)*

B. Was gefällt dir?   Several people are talking about what they like and don't like. For each sentence you hear, determine if the noun preceded by adjectives is masculine, neuter, feminine, or plural. You will hear each sentence twice.

BEISPIEL   Gemütliche, billige Lokale gefallen mir am besten.

	MASCULINE	NEUTER	FEMININE	PLURAL
Beispiel	_____	_____	_____	✓
1.	_____	_____	_____	_____
2.	_____	_____	_____	_____
3.	_____	_____	_____	_____
4.	_____	_____	_____	_____
5.	_____	_____	_____	_____
6.	_____	_____	_____	_____

Copyright © 1989 by Holt, Rinehart and Winston, Inc. All rights reserved.

*C. Das schmeckt mir nicht. Johannes's friend is making suggestions for dinner, but Johannes doesn't like any of the items mentioned. Give Johannes's answers to his friend's suggestions.

BEISPIEL   Bestell doch einen kalten Apfelsaft!
           Kalter Apfelsaft schmeckt mir nicht.

1   2   3   4   5   6   7   8

V. BAUSTEIN 9.4: <u>ABER</u> VS. <u>SONDERN</u>

A. . . . und Funktion *(Danke, aber . . .)*

B. Wir gehen aus! The Stifter and Keller families are out for the evening. The following sentences were taken from their conversation. For each sentence pair you hear, decide whether the conjunction **aber** or **sondern** best connects the two. Put a check mark in the appropriate column. You will hear each sentence pair twice.

BEISPIEL   Hilde möchte später ins Kino. Du möchtest ins Theater.

	ABER	**SONDERN**
Beispiel	✓	
1.		
2.		
3.		
4.		
5.		
6.		

C. Üben Sie! (Practice!) Connect the sentences with the conjunction you hear. Follow the model.

BEISPIEL   Harald hat das Pfeffersteak bestellt. Es hat ihm nicht geschmeckt. (aber)
           Harald hat das Pfeffersteak bestellt, aber es hat ihm nicht geschmeckt.

1   2   3   4   5   6

Copyright © 1989 by Holt, Rinehart and Winston, Inc. All rights reserved.

VI. SYNTHESE

A. Was mir schmeckt. Listen to what Herr Amsel has to say about his eating habits. You will then hear and see six incomplete statements about his comments. Indicate the correct ending to each sentence by circling the letter of the most appropriate response. Both the passage and the statements will be read twice.

1. Herr Amsel . . .
   a. ißt am liebsten in einfachen Gaststätten.
   b. ißt nie zu Hause.
   c. ißt gern einfaches Essen.
2. Herr Amsel sagt, daß . . .
   a. alle eleganten Gerichte französisch sind.
   b. elegante französische Gerichte ihm nicht gefallen.
   c. französische Namen ihm gefallen.
3. Herr Amsel ißt . . .
   a. nicht japanisches, sondern griechisches Essen.
   b. nie japanische oder griechische Gerichte.
   c. ungern japanisches Essen, denn es schmeckt ihm nicht.
4. Italienisches Essen . . .
   a. ißt Herr Amsel, aber es darf nichts Warmes sein.
   b. ißt Herr Amsel nie.
   c. hat Herr Amsel noch nie probiert.
5. Mann kann sagen, daß . . .
   a. Herr Amsel einen guten Appetit hat, denn er ißt viel.
   b. gute deutsche kalte Gerichte ihm am besten schmecken.
   c. er Salat und frisches Gemüse am liebsten ißt.

B. Schreiben Sie! Anneliese Dorn is talking about her restaurant, *Zur Grünen Laube.* During the pauses provided, write down what she says. Each sentence will be read a third time so that you can check what you've written.

1. _____

   _____

2. _____

   _____

3. _____

   _____

Copyright © 1989 by Holt, Rinehart and Winston, Inc. All rights reserved.

4. _____

_____

5. _____

_____

In 182 m Höhe dreht sich alles um den Gast

Ob ausgesuchtes Interieur, exzellenter Service oder Kochkunst der Spitzenklasse: im Olympiaturm-Drehrestaurant dreht sich alles um den Gast. Und der Gast dreht sich über allem, während er das beste aus Küche und Keller genießt.

Tel. 0 89/35 50 99

Drehrestaurant im Olympiaturm

PART TWO

I. BAUSTEIN 9.1: <u>LIEGEN</u>/(SICH) <u>LEGEN</u>; <u>SITZEN</u>/(SICH) <u>SETZEN</u>; <u>STEHEN/STELLEN</u>

So mußt du's machen.   Heinrich Blum is showing his son how to set a table. Using the correct form of **liegen, legen, stellen,** or **stehen,** complete his statements.

1. Zuerst mußt du eine Tischdecke auf den Tisch _____.

2. Gut. _____ jetzt die Blumen in die Mitte!

3. In Ordnung. Und wo _____ der Teller? Ja, richtig.

4. Und wo sollen der Löffel und die Gabel _____?

5. Gut gemacht! Und wo _____ die Tasse und Untertasse?

6. _____ die Serviette schon neben dem Teller? Nein, noch

    nicht. _____ sie daneben!

7. Und was brauchen wir noch? Richtig, jetzt _____ du das

    Messer rechts vom Teller.

8. Hast du auch schon den Brotteller auf den Tisch _____? So,

    jetzt können wir essen.

Copyright © 1989 by Holt, Rinehart and Winston, Inc. All rights reserved.   **159**

II. BAUSTEIN 9.2: ADJECTIVES AFTER EIN-WORDS

A. Große Pläne.   A group of students sitting in a **Beisel** are talking about their plans for the future. Complete their statements by filling in the appropriate *ein*-word and adjective endings.

1. Mein_____ groß_____ Traum ist ein_____ schön_____ Wohnung in der

   Stadt und ein_____ klein_____, gemütlich_____ Haus auf dem Land.

2. Ich möchte ein_____ beliebt_____ Sportler werden!

3. Wir sind realistischer! Susanne und ich freuen uns einfach auf

   unser_____ kurz_____ Reise in die Berge.

4. Ich möchte ein_____ attraktiv_____ Restaurant mit ein_____ ge-

   schmackvoll_____ Atmosphäre. Mein_____ viel_____ Gäste bringen

   ihr_____ best_____ Freunde, und . . .

5. Und ich baue ein_____ groß_____ Sportverein mit ein_____ herr-

   lich_____ Schwimmbad und ein_____ sehr schwer_____ Trimm-dich-

   Pfad *(masc.)*. Dann können dein_____ nett_____ Kunden *(customers)*

   mehr essen!

B. Auf der Wohnungssuche.   Elfriede and Heinz are looking at an apartment, but nothing about it seems to be right. Using the cues provided, recreate their statements.

Copyright © 1989 by Holt, Rinehart and Winston, Inc. All rights reserved.

1. Was? Diese Wohnung hat _____ _____ Eßzim-

   mer? *(no bigger)*

2. So _____ _____ Küche gefällt mir nicht. *(an*

   old-fashioned)

3. Ich möchte lieber _____ _____ Balkon! *(a nicer)*

4. Ein Rockstar wohnt in diesem Haus? Ich will aber _____

   _____ Nachbarn! *(a quiet)*

5. Wir brauchen aber _____ _____ Arbeitszimmer.

   (a more comfortable)

6. Wir möchten in _____ _____ Gegend wohnen.

   (a safer)

7. Wir gehen abends gern aus. Gibt es _____ _____

   Kneipe in der Nähe? *(no cozy)*

8. Nein, in so _____ _____ Wohnung können wir

   nicht wohnen! *(a dark)*

III. BAUSTEIN 9.3: UNPRECEDED ATTRIBUTIVE ADJECTIVES

A. „Der Goldene Topf".   A group of friends are arguing about a
well-known restaurant in town. Using the cues provided, recreate their
statements.

1. _____ *(Good)* Freunde haben mir erzählt, es gibt

   _____ *(excellent)* Essen im „Goldenen Topf".

Copyright © 1989 by Holt, Rinehart and Winston, Inc. All rights reserved.

2. Das ist _____ _____ (nothing new). Diese

   Gaststätte existiert schon seit _____ (many) Jahren.

3. Aber _____ _____ (many/other) Leute sagen,

   daß _____ _____ (a few/Italian) Gerichte

   gar nicht schmecken.

4. Dann muß man _____ _____ (something

   German) bestellen. Es gibt _____ _____

   _____ (a lot of good German) Spezialitäten auf der Speise-

   karte.

5. Aber es gibt _____ (nothing that's fresh).

6. Was? Ich esse dort immer _____ (fresh) Gemüse, und

   _____ (homemade) Wurst gibt es auch täglich.

7. Aber ich meine, es gibt _____ und _____

   (better/cheaper) Restaurants.

BERLIN? – HOTEL BERLIN!

IHR KINDERFREUNDLICHES HOTEL

Familienknüller

Spaghetti ohne Ende

vom reichhaltigen Büfett
Sonntag, 11. 10. 87

DM 9,50 Preis pro Person

Pro zahlender Gast ißt 1 Kind bis zu 12 Jahren
die Spaghetti gratis! Tischreservierungen erbeten.

. . . Am 18. 10. 87 Barbecue-Leckereien
von 12.00–15.00 Uhr, Preis pro Person: 26,50.
Es gilt unser kinderfreundliches Angebot

HOTEL BERLIN

HOTEL BERLIN

Lützowplatz 17, 1000 Berlin 30
☎ (030) 26 05-0, Tx 184 332

Copyright © 1989 by Holt, Rinehart and Winston, Inc. All rights reserved.

B. Und Sie? Complete the following sentences with whatever adjectives or series of adjectives you find appropriate.

1. Ich interessiere mich nicht für _____ Filme.

2. _____ Wetter gefällt mir (nicht).

3. Ich ärgere mich über _____ Professoren.

4. Meine Freunde sehen oft _____ Fernsehsendungen.

5. Ich esse am liebsten in _____ Gaststätten.

6. Ich spreche gern mit _____ Menschen.

7. Eine Kneipe mit _____ Atmosphäre gefällt mir (nicht).

8. Mein(e) ideale(r) Partner(in) hat _____ Augen und

_____ Haar.

IV. BAUSTEIN 9.4: ABER VS. SONDERN

A. Aber oder sondern? Describe the day's activities for this group of German students on vacation. Complete the sentences by using the following elements and the conjunction **aber** or **sondern**.

BEISPIEL   Edith will heute abend nicht zu Hause arbeiten. Sie will später ausgehen.
Edith will heute abend nicht zu Hause arbeiten, sondern will später ausgehen.

a. Annette hat drei Museen besucht.
b. Sie ist gegangen.
c. Ich gehe gern mit dir zum Weinfest.
d. Ich will keinen Wein trinken.

e. Er hat ein großes Frühstück gehabt.
f. Er hat ihnen ein Telegramm geschickt.
g. Sie hat ein Taxi genommen.

1. Anneliese ist nicht mit der U-Bahn zum Zoo gefahren, _____

_____.

2. Ich gehe heute abend zum Weinfest, _____

_____.

Copyright © 1989 by Holt, Rinehart and Winston, Inc. All rights reserved.

3. Ulf ist den ganzen Tag im Hotel geblieben, _____

   _____ .

4. Inge hat sich nicht auf das Weinfest gefreut, _____

   _____ .

5. Ich habe eigentlich keine Zeit, _____

   _____ .

6. Albert hat heute nicht zu Mittag gegessen, _____

   _____ .

7. David hat seine Eltern nicht angerufen, _____

   _____ .

B. Das Tagebuch.   Larry, an American student, is keeping a diary during his stay in Switzerland. Improve the German style in this diary entry by using **und, aber, oder, sondern,** or **denn** to form compound sentences. Use a separate piece of paper.

Heute morgen bin ich früh aufgestanden. Ich habe vor dem Frühstück eine Stunde Tennis gespielt. Dann habe ich zum Frühstück zwei Eier gegessen. Ich habe eine Tasse Kaffee getrunken. Ich habe nicht die Zeitung gelesen. Ich habe die Nachrichten im Fernsehen gesehen. Danach bin ich zur Bank und zur Drogerie gegangen. Ich mußte Geld wechseln. Ich mußte Seife und Zahnpasta kaufen. Später bin ich zu Fuß durch die ganze Stadt gelaufen. Ich habe mir die schönen Häuser und Kirchen angesehen. Ich bin gar nicht müde geworden. Ich habe mich danach sehr wohl gefühlt. Zu Abend habe ich mit Freunden in einem netten Gasthaus gegessen. Ich habe Bratwurst und Sauerkraut probiert. Es hat mir leider nicht geschmeckt. Danach sind wir alle zu einer Diskothek gegangen. Wir wollten tanzen. Jetzt bin ich müde. Ich freue mich schon auf morgen.

V. SYNTHESE

A. Im Restaurant.   In a restaurant you overhear fragments of the following dialogue between the waiter and a customer. Supply the missing half of the exchange.

Copyright © 1989 by Holt, Rinehart and Winston, Inc. All rights reserved.

Ober: _____

Kunde *(customer):* Was empfehlen Sie, Herr Ober?

Ober: _____

Kunde: Ich habe großen Hunger.

Ober: _____

     (Ein wenig später . . .)

Kunde: _____

Ober: Hat's geschmeckt? Das macht zusammen 15 Mark 80.

Kunde: _____

B. Ein Feinschmecker berichtet. (A gourmet reports.) Imagine that you are a restaurant reviewer for a gourmet magazine. Write a review of a restaurant or café, real or fictitious. Describe in detail your experience at the restaurant: the atmosphere, how the food was served, the other patrons, and the cuisine. Remember that your readers expect a review that reflects your eminently good taste and exacting standards. Use a separate piece of paper.

Copyright © 1989 by Holt, Rinehart and Winston, Inc. All rights reserved.

Restaurant

Isi's Goldener Engel

Im Herzen von Garmisch
Am Marienplatz · Tel. 08821/56677

Wild- und Fischspezialitäten
Bayerische Schmankerl
Bayer. Bierstüberl täglich ab 17.00 Uhr geöffnet

Konditorei - Café
8100 GARMISCH-PARTENKIRCHEN — Zugspitzstraße 106
Telefon (08821) 56315
Was wir als zweitältestes Konditorei-Café an bestem Kaffee,
feinsten Torten und Kuchen bieten, ist einen Besuch wert.
Montag Ruhetag · Parkplatz · Garten-Terrasse

KAPITEL **10 DIE WELT VON MORGEN**

PART ONE

I. UND SIE?

Probleme überall. Listen as citizens talk about some problems or issues that concern them. After each person speaks, you will hear two questions in German. Circle the letter of the best answer to each question. You will hear each person speak twice.

1. Was hält Frau Langnese für das größte Problem?
   a. eine aggressive Regierung   b. die Zerstörung des Waldes   c. Umweltverschmutzung
2. Wofür hält Frau Langnese das Problem?
   a. für unnötig   b. für ernst   c. für hoffnungslos
3. Worum macht sich Frau Doktor Werner die meisten Sorgen?
   a. Luft- und Wasserverschmutzung   b. die Zerstörung der Tier- und Pflanzenwelt   c. den sauren Regen
4. Was ist für Frau Doktor Werner eine Lösung?
   a. nicht aufgeben   b. nicht daran denken   c. nichts dagegen tun
5. Was hält Herr Langer für die größte Gefahr?
   a. die Luftverschmutzung   b. das Gift im Essen   c. die Zerstörung der Umwelt
6. Was ist für Herrn Langer eine Lösung?
   a. darüber diskutieren   b. dagegen kämpfen   c. es unnötig finden

II. BAUSTEIN 10.1: FUTURE TENSE

A. . . . und Funktion *(Der Umweltfreund.)*

B. Meine Damen und Herren! Richard is practicing a speech he is to give at an environmental rally. For each sentence you hear, decide

Copyright © 1989 by Holt, Rinehart and Winston, Inc. All rights reserved.

whether the verb **werden** is used as the future auxiliary or whether it means "become." Put a check mark under the appropriate column. You will hear each sentence twice.

BEISPIEL   Unsere Welt kann und muß sauberer und sicherer werden.

	FUTURE TENSE	**BECOME**
Beispiel	_____	___✓___
1.	_____	_____
2.	_____	_____
3.	_____	_____
4.	_____	_____
5.	_____	_____
6.	_____	_____

*C. Nächstes Jahr . . .   Many people make plans and resolutions at the beginning of a new year. Using the cues, tell what the following people say.

BEISPIEL   Herr Bartels: nicht so viel arbeiten
Ich werde nicht so viel arbeiten.

1   2   3   4   5   6   7   8

III. BAUSTEIN 10.2: INFINITIVES WITH ZU

A. . . . und Funktion *(Nichts zu diskutieren!)*

B. Was meinen Sie?   Listen as several people comment on a recent energy policy announcement made by their government. After each person speaks, you will hear a question about what the person said. Stop the tape and write your answer to the question, using an infinitive phrase. You will hear each passage and question twice.

Copyright © 1989 by Holt, Rinehart and Winston, Inc. All rights reserved.   **168**

BEISPIEL. Herr Jünger: Na ja, so ist's immer. So viel Verschwendung in der Regierung und in der Industrie . . . Und die Bürger sollen die Verantwortung tragen. Höhere Preise für Benzin? Nein, die bezahle ich einfach nicht!

Wofür interessiert sich Herr Jünger gar nicht?
Höhere Preise für Benzin zu bezahlen.

1. Was findet Frau Schultz gar nicht leicht? _____

_____

2. Wofür sind strengere Gesetze die beste Lösung? _____

_____

3. Was soll die Regierung versuchen? _____

_____

*C. Gründe. There is a reason for everything, and Helmut seems to know what it is. Using the cues, give Helmut's answers to his friends' questions.

BEISPIEL   Warum reißt man die alte Post ab? (einen Parkplatz bauen)
Man reißt die alte Post ab, um einen Parkplatz zu bauen.

1   2   3   4   5   6   7   8

IV. BAUSTEIN 10.3: PRESENT PERFECT OF MODAL VERBS

A. . . . und Funktion (*Hochhäuser oder Sanierung?*)

B. Der Aktivist.   The Lohnes's are discussing with their son Dieter his participation in recent antinuclear activities. Listen to what each person says, and decide if the modal verb in each sentence is in the present tense, the present perfect, or the future tense. Indicate your answer with a check mark in the appropriate column. You will hear each sentence twice.

Copyright © 1989 by Holt, Rinehart and Winston, Inc. All rights reserved.

BEISPIEL   Ach, Dieter, warum hast du gegen die Regierung kämpfen wollen?

	PRESENT	PRESENT PERFECT	FUTURE
Beispiel	_____	____✓____	_____
1.	_____	_____	_____
2.	_____	_____	_____
3.	_____	_____	_____
4.	_____	_____	_____
5.	_____	_____	_____
6.	_____	_____	_____

C. Eine Bürgerinitiative.   Helena is inquiring about a citizen's action group that is responsible for many changes in their town. Use the cues to tell how a city council member answers her questions.

BEISPIEL   Warum hat man das Gebäude saniert?   (vor der Zerstörung retten wollen)
Man hat es vor der Zerstörung retten wollen.

1   2   3   4   5

V.   BAUSTEIN 10.4: SUBORDINATING CONJUNCTIONS

A. . . . und Funktion *(Und die nächste Generation?)*

B. Das wollen wir nicht!   The citizens of a small rural community are disturbed because the nearby big city is expanding in their direction. They air their concerns at a meeting with officials from the big city. Listen as each person speaks, then complete the statements by circling the letter of the correct choice from the alternatives given. You will hear each speaker twice.

1. Streets and streetcar lines will have to be built . . .
    a. after they build the second factory.
    b. while a second factory, a supermarket and high-rise buildings are being built.
    c. before the first factory is built.

Copyright © 1989 by Holt, Rinehart and Winston, Inc. All rights reserved.

2. In this speaker's opinion, people will see the negative side of progress . . .
   a. when citizens no longer fight against it.
   b. whenever politicians have big plans.
   c. as soon as there are big parking lots instead of playgrounds everywhere.
3. The speaker will probably leave this community and move further into the country . . .
   a. even though her family just recently moved here.
   b. to live in quieter surroundings.
   c. since now there is water pollution here, too.

C. Retten wir die Tiere!   Roberta is a member of an activist group that hopes to save wild animals and their environments. To tell what she says, connect each pair of sentences you hear with the conjunction indicated in your lab manual.

BEISPIEL   Retten wir die Tiere. Es ist zu spät. (bevor)
Retten wir die Tiere, bevor es zu spät ist.

1. wenn   2. bis   3. damit   4. daß

Now begin each pair of sentences by putting the indicated conjunction at the start.

BEISPIEL   Ich mache mir große Sorgen. Ich bin in diesem Verein aktiv. (da)
Da ich mir große Sorgen mache, bin ich in diesem Verein aktiv.

5. während   6. sobald   7. nachdem   8. seitdem

VI.   SYNTHESE

A. Mein liebes Kind!   Listen as Annette Anton, a political activist, and her more conservative father discuss Annette's interest in politics. You will then hear five statements. Circle **richtig** if the sentence is true and **falsch** if it is false. Both the passage and the statements will be read twice.

1. richtig   falsch   2. richtig   falsch
3. richtig   falsch   4. richtig   falsch
5. richtig   falsch

B. Persönliche Fragen.   Listen to the following four questions. After each question there will be a pause so that you can answer in complete sentences. Each question will be asked twice.

1   2   3   4

Copyright © 1989 by Holt, Rinehart and Winston, Inc. All rights reserved.

PART TWO

I. BAUSTEIN 10.1: FUTURE TENSE

A. Ein Traum. Annette Müller has had a dream in which she saw the future course of her life and that of her friends. She is sharing her dream with them. Following the model and using the appropriate form of the future tense, recreate her statements.

BEISPIEL   Johanna: du/machen/ein- groß- Reise/um die Welt
  Johanna, du wirst eine große Reise um die Welt machen.

1. Jakob: du/haben/groß- Angst/vor Technologie

    _____

2. Roboter/spielen/ein- groß- Rolle/in unser- Leben

    _____

3. ich/müssen/sich/ein- neu- Arbeitsplatz/suchen//denn/ich/können/nicht mehr/bei Lebensmittelgeschäft Kupsch/arbeiten

    _____

    _____

    _____

4. Christel und Jochen: ihr/werden/berühmt- Politiker

    _____

5. wir/lösen/all- schwer- Probleme/allein//und/retten/die Welt

    _____

    _____

Copyright © 1989 by Holt, Rinehart and Winston, Inc. All rights reserved.

B. Astrologie. Imagine you are an astrologer who is making predictions. Complete the statements, using the appropriate form of the future tense.

1. Unsere Regierung _____

2. Computer _____

3. Die Politiker unserer Nation _____

4. Unsere Städte _____

5. Mein(e) Deutschprofessor(in) _____

II. BAUSTEIN 10.2: INFINITIVES WITH ZU

A. Idealistisch oder zynisch.   Public opinion can range from the idealistic to the cynical. Complete the following dialogue by choosing an appropriate verb from among those listed. Be sure to use **zu** and the infinitive form of the verb.

VERBEN: **verbringen, lösen, finden, zusammenarbeiten, verschwenden, entwickeln, schützen, kämpfen, sparen, leben, ausgeben, sein**

1. Frau Grüne: Wir dürfen es nicht aufgeben, für unsere Ideale

    _____ .

    Herr Spießer: Ich finde es nutzlos, so idealistisch _____ .

2. Frau Grüne: Um die Natur _____ , brauchen wir strengere Gesetze.

    Herr Spießer: Ich halte es aber für unmöglich, mit der Regierung

    _____ .

3. Frau Grüne: Wir tun noch nicht genug, Energiealternativen

    _____ .

    Herr Spießer: Ich finde es unnötig, so viel Geld für solche Alternativen

    _____ .

Copyright © 1989 by Holt, Rinehart and Winston, Inc. All rights reserved.

4. Frau Grüne: Um gesünder und länger _____, sollen die

Menschen nicht so viel Auto fahren.

Herr Spießer: Um unsere Wirtschaftsprobleme _____,

müssen wir aber mehr Autos bauen.

5. Frau Grüne: Wir dürfen es nicht aufgeben, bessere Lösungen

_____.

Herr Spießer: Ich halte es für unpraktisch, so viel Zeit damit

_____.

6. Frau Grüne: Um weniger Energie _____, brauchen wir

strengere Gesetze.

Herr Spießer: Um mehr Energie _____, sollen die

Preise dafür viel höher sein.

B. Und was meinen Sie? Complete the following sentences with an infinitive phrase, to show your opinion on various trends and attitudes.

1. Viele Städte retten jetzt ihre alten Gebäude, um _____

_____.

2. Unser Land fängt jetzt an, _____

_____.

3. Viele Bürger haben Angst, _____

_____.

4. Einige Menschen verlassen die Großstädte, um _____

_____.

Copyright © 1989 by Holt, Rinehart and Winston, Inc. All rights reserved. **175**

5. Manche Bürger haben nie Zeit, _____

_____ .

6. Wir müssen alle zusammenarbeiten, um _____

_____ .

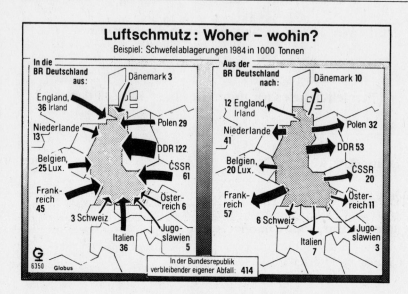

III. BAUSTEIN 10.3: PRESENT PERFECT OF MODAL VERBS

Früher. Choosing from among the following suggestions, create eight sentences in the present perfect that are true statements about your past or that of your family or friends.

BEISPIEL   im Fernsehen nicht sehen dürfen
   Ich habe früher nie Krimis im Fernsehen sehen dürfen.

im Kino sehen können
nicht machen können
immer besuchen wollen
im Fernsehen nicht sehen dürfen
am Sonntag machen wollen
am Samstag tun müssen

nicht kaufen dürfen
helfen sollen
kaufen wollen
nie essen wollen
umziehen müssen
??

Copyright © 1989 by Holt, Rinehart and Winston, Inc. All rights reserved.

1. _____

_____

2. _____

_____

3. _____

_____

4. _____

_____

5. _____

_____

6. _____

_____

7. _____

_____

8. _____

_____

IV. BAUSTEIN 10.4: SUBORDINATING CONJUNCTIONS

A. Ich mache mir Sorgen. Irmgard is a concerned environmentalist who has been asked to write an article about the current situation. Choose an appropriate conjunction to combine the pairs of sentences below so as to tell what Irmgard writes.

Copyright © 1989 by Holt, Rinehart and Winston, Inc. All rights reserved.

CONJUNCTIONS: **ob, obwohl, da, bevor, sobald, bis, während, damit, seitdem, nachdem**

BEISPIEL   Wir müssen jetzt dagegen demonstrieren. Unsere Kinder können besser leben.
Damit unsere Kinder besser leben können, müssen wir jetzt dagegen demonstrieren.

1.   Viele wollen wissen. Das neue Programm wird Erfolg haben.

_____

_____

2.   Man kann hier nicht mehr schwimmen. Es gibt Chemikalien im Wasser.

_____

_____

3.   Manche Politiker sprechen von einer hoffnungsvollen Zukunft. Andere sprechen von einer Katastrophe.

_____

_____

4.   Alle Bürger interessieren sich für ihre Umwelt. Wir werden die Natur nicht schützen können.

_____

_____

5.   Viele Leute wollen nicht aktiv werden. Die Natur und unsere Städte sind schon in Gefahr.

_____

_____

B. Meinungen über die Zukunft.   Complete the following sentences by stating your opinion.

Copyright © 1989 by Holt, Rinehart and Winston, Inc. All rights reserved.   **178**

1. Viele Leute verschwenden sehr viel Energie, obwohl _____

_____ .

2. Während manche Bürger sich Sorgen um die Zukunft machen, _____

_____ .

3. Bevor man zu pessimistisch wird, _____

_____ .

4. Seitdem wir großen Fortschritt in der Technologie gemacht haben, _____

_____ .

5. Da der saure Regen schon ein großes Problem ist, _____

_____ .

6. Ich frage mich, ob _____

_____ .

V. SYNTHESE

Leserbriefe. (Letters to the editor.) Choose one of the cartoons below as the basis for an open letter addressed to a newspaper. Take a strong position and express your reactions and views on the issue. Use a separate piece of paper for your letter.

Copyright © 1989 by Holt, Rinehart and Winston, Inc. All rights reserved.

Copyright © 1989 by Holt, Rinehart and Winston, Inc. All rights reserved.

Copyright © 1989 by Holt, Rinehart and Winston, Inc. All rights reserved.

Copyright © 1989 by Holt, Rinehart and Winston, Inc. All rights reserved.

KAPITEL 11 GESTERN UND HEUTE

PART ONE

I. UND SIE?

Zu welcher Gelegenheit? (On which occasion?) Listen to the following excerpts from conversations, then write in the spaces provided the name of the holiday or occasion about which the people are speaking. You will hear each conversation twice.

BEISPIEL   Sigrid und Hans! Wir gratulieren. Nun wann, sagt ihr, ist die Hochzeit?
Wir planen, am Samstag vor Ostern zu heiraten.
Ach, wie schön. Wir freuen uns schon darauf.

Weihnachten   Geburtsag
Ostern
Reise   Krankheit
Verlobung
Hochzeitsjubiläum
Hochzeit   Silvester

Beispiel   __ Verlobung __

1. _____   2. _____

3. _____   4. _____

5. _____

Copyright © 1989 by Holt, Rinehart and Winston, Inc. All rights reserved.   **183**

II. BAUSTEIN 11.1: SIMPLE PAST OF REGULAR AND MIXED VERBS

A. **. . . und Funktion** *(Das war peinlich!)*

B. Im Fotoalbum. Listen as Johann and Karin read the captions from their aunt's photo album. Decide whether what they read is in the present tense or in the simple past tense. Put a check mark in the appropriate column to indicate your answer. Each sentence will be read twice.

BEISPIEL   1948. Unsere Verlobung. Wir heiraten im Dezember!

	PRESENT	SIMPLE PAST
Beispiel	✓	
1.		
2.		
3.		
4.		
5.		
6.		

*C. Aber er . . . Herr König hasn't been very popular at the office lately and his employees are complaining about him. Use the cues to tell what they say.

Copyright © 1989 by Holt, Rinehart and Winston, Inc. All rights reserved.

BEISPIEL   Gestern mußten wir arbeiten. (mit seinem Computer spielen)
. . . aber er spielte mit seinem Computer.

1   2   3 · 4   5   6   7

III. BAUSTEIN 11.2: SIMPLE PAST OF IRREGULAR VERBS

A. . . . und Funktion *(Eine Frage der Perspektive.)*

B. Im Urlaub.   Listen as Anneliese tells about a childhood vacation trip. You will hear the entire passage once. Then you will hear one sentence at a time. Write the infinitive of the verb or verbs in each sentence in the spaces provided.

BEISPIEL   Ich fand unseren Urlaub in der Schweiz phantastisch.

Beispiel __finden__

1. _____   2. _____

3. _____   4. _____

5. _____   6. _____

7. _____

*C. Die Faschingzeit.   Willi and Roberta are recalling last year's Fasching activities. Tell what they say by forming sentences in the simple past from the cues.

BEISPIEL   die Party: um acht Uhr beginnen
Die Party begann um acht Uhr.

1   2   3   4   5   6   7   8   9   10

IV. BAUSTEIN 11.3: ORDINAL NUMBERS

A. . . . und Funktion *(Weißt du's?)*

B. Am wievielten?   Ingrid works in a busy florist's shop. Listen as customers order flowers for various occasions and record in English in the spaces provided the information she writes down. Each order will be read twice.

Copyright © 1989 by Holt, Rinehart and Winston, Inc. All rights reserved.   **185**

BEISPIEL   Klara Schiller, Hauptstraße 14.
    Am 15. Mai feiert sie ihren 16. Geburtstag.

Beispiel   Name: Klara Schiller
        Occasion: 16th birthday
        Date: May 15
        Address: Hauptstraße 14

1. Name: Ingeborg Schmidt

   Occasion: _____

   Date: _____

   Address: _____

2. Name: Karl und Leona Reidt

   Occasion: _____

   Date: _____

   Address: _____

3. Name: Herbert und Judith

         Marcuse

   Occasion: _____

   Date: _____

   Address: _____

4. Name: Christoph Eschenbach

   Occasion: _____

   Date: _____

   Address: _____

5. Name: Elfriede Baumann

   Occasion: _____

   Date: _____

   Address: _____

6. Name: Paul Klein

   Occasion: _____

   Date: _____

   Address: _____

*C. Omas Dachboden.   (Grandma's attic.) As Oma Schürz shows Karl-Heinz and Inge some things from a trunk in her attic, they ask her questions about the past. Use the cues to tell how she answers.

BEISPIEL   Wann bekam Onkel Heinrich diesen Löffel? *(for his second birthday)*
    Zu seinem zweiten Geburtstag.

1   2   3   4   5   6   7   8

Copyright © 1989 by Holt, Rinehart and Winston, Inc. All rights reserved.

V. BAUSTEIN 11.4: <u>ALS</u>, <u>WENN</u>, <u>WANN</u>

A. . . . und Funktion *(Das Klassenfest.)*

B. Wenn . . . People from different generations and places were interviewed for a newspaper article entitled **Traditionen: Vergangenheit und Zukunft.** Listen to some of their comments, and decide for each excerpt whether the word **wenn** refers to a recurring event or the future or if it has the meaning "if." Put a check mark under the appropriate column. You will hear each excerpt twice.

BEISPIEL   Mein Onkel Felix ist immer sehr stolz, wenn man von den Bräuchen unserer Gegend spricht.

	RECURRING EVENT	**FUTURE**	**IF**
Beispiel	✓		
1.			
2.			
3.			
4.			
5.			
6.			

C. Ich erinnere mich daran . . . Several old friends are talking about mutual friends and shared experiences. Combine each pair of sentences with **als, wenn,** or **wann** to tell what they say.

BEISPIEL   Wir haben Robert besser kennengelernt. Er verbrachte einen Sommer bei uns.
Wir haben Robert besser kennengelernt, als er einen Sommer bei uns verbrachte.

1   2   3   4   5   6

Copyright © 1989 by Holt, Rinehart and Winston, Inc. All rights reserved.   **187**

VI. SYNTHESE

A. Unsere Bräuche.   Listen as a tourist guide in Nürnberg explains some national and local customs to a German-speaking visitor. You will then hear six statements. Given what she has just said, decide whether she is likely to have made the statements to a subsequent visitor. Circle **ja** if she might have made the statement or **nein** if she would not have. Both the passage and the statements will be read twice.

1. Der moderne Mensch feiert heute weniger. ja nein
2. Persönliche Feste spielen eine genauso große Rolle wie nationale Feiertage. ja nein
3. Den 1. Mai feiert man überall in der Bundesrepublik. ja nein
4. Der Fasching ist ein lustiges Volksfest. ja nein
5. In der ganzen Bundersrepublik beginnt der Fasching am 11. November. ja nein
6. Eine ziemlich neue Tradition ist der Christkindlmarkt in Nürnberg. ja nein

B. Persönliche Fragen.   Listen to the following four questions. After each question there will be a pause so that you can write down your answer in complete sentences. After all the questions have been asked they will be read again, so that you may check what you've written.

1. _____

_____

2. _____

_____

3. _____

_____

4. _____

_____

Copyright © 1989 by Holt, Rinehart and Winston, Inc. All rights reserved.

PART TWO

I. BAUSTEIN 11.1: SIMPLE PAST OF REGULAR AND MIXED VERBS

A. Es war einmal . . . (Once upon a time . . .) Opa Eisenstein is entertaining his two grandchildren with a fairy tale. Using the cues provided, recreate his narrative in the simple past.

„Ein kleines Mädchen und ihre Mutter _____ *(lived)* in

einem kleinen Haus am Wald. Eines Tages _____ *(said)*

die Mutter, daß das Mädchen ihre liebe Großmutter besuchen

_____ *(should)*. Die Großmutter _____

(felt) sich nicht wohl und _____ *(spent)* Tag und Nacht im

Bett. Die Mutter _____ *(put)* Brot und eine Flasche Wein

in einen Korb *(basket)*. Das Mädchen _____ *(knew)*, daß

die Großmutter auf der anderen Seite des Waldes _____

(lived), aber es _____ *(had)* keine Angst. Es

_____ *(loved)* den dunklen Wald und

_____ *(knew)* ihn gut.

„Auf dem Weg *(way)* _____ *(thought)* das Mädchen

immer an die kranke Großmutter und _____ *(looked*

forward to) den Besuch. Aber plötzlich: ein großer Wolf! Er

_____ *(asked)* das Mädchen: ‚Wohin gehst du?' Das

Mädchen _____ *(answered)* . . . Aber wie geht die Ge-

Copyright © 1989 by Holt, Rinehart and Winston, Inc. All rights reserved. **189**

schichte zu Ende? _____ *(did know)* ihr die ganze Zeit,

wer das Mädchen ist?"

,,Natürlich, Opa! Rotkäppchen!"

B. Was ich letzten Sommer machte.   Susan had to write an essay
for her German class about what she did last summer. Choosing from
the following list of verbs, recreate her narrative in the simple past.
Use each verb only once.

VERBEN: **arbeiten**   **sich gewöhnen**   **tanzen**
           beantworten   **sich interessieren**   **übernachten**
           brauchen   **kennenlernen**   **verbringen**
           dauern   **machen**   **verdienen**
           einkaufen   **mieten**   **wandern**
           sich entspannen   **spielen**
           erzählen   **studieren**
           sich freuen   **suchen**

Letzten Frühling _____ ich mir einen Sommerjob, denn

ich _____ und _____ mehr Geld. Meine

Freunde _____ mir über ein Hotel in den Bergen, und ich

_____ _____ sofort dafür. Das Hotel

_____ auch bald meinen Brief. Der Job

_____ drei Monate und ich konnte im Juni damit beginnen.

Einige Studenten aus dem Ausland _____ auch dort, und

ich _____ viele interessante Leute

_____. Obwohl wir nicht viel Geld

_____, _____ uns die Arbeit Spaß. Wir

_____ _____ schnell an die tägliche Routine, aber ich

_____ _____ auch immer über ein freies Wochenende.

Copyright © 1989 by Holt, Rinehart and Winston, Inc. All rights reserved.

Während einige Touristen nur im Hotel _____,

_____ viele Gäste zwei bis drei Wochen da. Während des

Tages _____ sie dann oder _____ Tennis,

_____ Fahrräder oder _____ in den

vielen netten kleinen Boutiquen _____. Am Abend

_____ sie im großen Tanzsaal (ballroom) oder

_____ _____ auf der Terrasse. Ich muß sagen, manch-

mal wollte ich Gast sein, nicht Kellnerin!

II. BAUSTEIN 11.2: SIMPLE PAST OF IRREGULAR VERBS

A. Erinnerungen an die Vergangenheit. Kathrin and Julian are reminiscing about their childhood. Complete their story by giving the appropriate form of the simple past for the verbs in parentheses.

KATHRIN: Als ich ein Kind _____ (sein),

_____ (halten) ich meine Geburtstagsfeiern für besonders

schön. Meine Eltern _____ alle meine kleinen Freunde

_____ (einladen), und wir _____ (essen) viel Kuchen und

_____ (trinken) schrecklich viel heiße Schokolade. Natürlich

_____ (bekommen) wir alle Bauchweh danach! Es

_____ (geben) großen Lärm im Haus. Und mir

_____ (gefallen) die vielen schönen Geschenke.

JULIAN: Als Kind _____ (halten) ich die Osterzeit für

sehr schön. Nach dem langen kalten Winter _____ (kommen)

Copyright © 1989 by Holt, Rinehart and Winston, Inc. All rights reserved.

der Frühling endlich wieder. Wir _____ (tragen) keine

schweren Mäntel mehr und das _____ (gefallen) mir. An

Ostern _____ dann die ganze Familie im Wald

_____ (spazierengehen). Meine Mutter

_____ (vorschlagen), Ostereier zu suchen. Wir Kinder

_____ (laufen) durch den ganzen Wald und

_____ (finden) viele Schokoladeneier im Gras. Wir

_____ (sein) glücklich.

B. Ein Interview.   Imagine that you are going to interview a Swiss
senior citizen to find out what life was like when he or she was growing
up. Using the **Sie** form and the simple past, how would you ask the
following questions?

1. Was there always enough time for your hobbies? (Use *geben.*) _____

    _____

2. Did you often go to the movies and the theater with your friends?

    _____

    _____

3. Where and when did the most meaningful family celebration in your

    family take place? _____

    _____

4. When did you leave your family? _____

    _____

5. Which customs did you like best of all? (Use *gefallen.*) _____

    _____

Copyright © 1989 by Holt, Rinehart and Winston, Inc. All rights reserved.

III. BAUSTEIN 11.3: ORDINAL NUMBERS

A. Ein Jahr im Leben der Familie Kröger. Use the cues to answer the questions below.

BEISPIEL   Wann fand das Richtfest statt? (31.5.)
   am einunddreißigsten Mai

1. Wann heirateten Inge und Jens? (3.4.)

   _____

2. Wann fand Herrn und Frau Krögers fünfundzwanzigstes Hochzeitsjubiläum statt? (1.10.)

   _____

3. Wann fuhr die Familie aufs Land? (7.7.–30.7.)

   _____

4. Wann war Alberts erster Schultag? (28.8.)

   _____

5. Wann feierten die Kinder Fasching? (18.2)

   _____

6. Wann machte Stephanie ihren Führerschein? (23.5.)

   _____

B. Wie sagt man . . . ? Give the German equivalent for the following.

1. for the fifth time _____

2. in the twentieth century _____

3. June first _____

4. my eighteenth birthday _____

Copyright © 1989 by Holt, Rinehart and Winston, Inc. All rights reserved.

IV. BAUSTEIN 11.4: <u>ALS</u>, <u>WENN</u>, <u>WANN</u>

A. Bedeutungsvolle Erlebnisse. Lisa heard a group of Germans talk about some important experiences in their childhood. Use **als, wenn,** or **wann** to recreate their statements.

1. _____ ich noch jünger war, freute ich mich sehr auf die Weih-

   nachtszeit. Aber ich glaube, ich hatte immer sehr viel Angst,

   _____ der Nikolaus am sechsten Dezember vor der Tür stand.

2. _____ das Wetter schön war, durften wir immer lang mit den

   Nachbarskindern auf der Straße spielen. _____ dann der Winter

   kam, war diese herrliche Zeit vorbei.

3. Ich war immer sehr glücklich, _____ unsere Cousins und Ku-

   sinen zu Besuch kamen. Sie brachten immer so schöne Spielzeuge *(toys)*

   mit.

4. _____ Sie mich fragen, welches Erlebnis für mich das bedeu-

Copyright © 1989 by Holt, Rinehart and Winston, Inc. All rights reserved.   **194**

tungsvollste war, kann ich Ihnen nicht antworten. Jeder Tag war eigent-

lich interessant für mich!

5. Ich habe vergessen, _____ meine Tante geheiratet hat. Aber ich

erinnere mich an ihr langes weißes Kleid.

6. Ich liebte Trickfilme, _____ ich ein Kind war. _____ ich

meinen siebten Geburtstag feierte, durfte ich meine Freunde ins Kino

einladen — das war toll!

Musikfreunde

Gezeichnet
von Renate Alf

B. In der DDR.   Imagine that you want to observe and record some
of the customs in the DDR. Using the **Sie** form, ask the following
questions in German.

1. When you have a vacation, where do you go?

_____

2. If you stay at home, what do you do in your leisure time?

_____

_____

3. When your children were young, how did you spend the Christmas
holidays?

_____

_____

Copyright © 1989 by Holt, Rinehart and Winston, Inc. All rights reserved.

4. When did you get married?

_____

5. Are there special *(besondere)* customs when one gets married in the DDR?

_____

_____

V.   SYNTHESE

A. Bräuche und Feste.   Referring to the **Land und Leute** section in your textbook on customs and holidays, answer the following questions with complete sentences.

1. Wenn man zu einem berühmten Christkindlmarkt gehen will, welche Städte besucht man?

_____

2. Was ist der Namenstag? _____

_____

3. Wo findet die Fastnacht statt, und was ist typisch dafür? _____

_____

_____

4. Was ist ein besonderes Ereignis im Spätwinter in Österreich und in den katholischen Gegenden Deutschlands? Was tut man da? _____

_____

_____

B. BRD und DDR —— die ersten 40 Jahre.   On a separate piece of paper, write a paragraph based on the **Land und Leute** section in your textbook about the development of the two German states. Be sure to address the following questions:

Copyright © 1989 by Holt, Rinehart and Winston, Inc. All rights reserved.

NAME _____ DATE _____ CLASS _____

1. Wie viele Zonen gab es im Jahr 1945?
2. In welchem Jahr gab es dann zwei deutsche Nationen?
3. Wann wurde die BRD ein Mitglied der NATO?
4. Wann gründete *(founded)* man die EWG?
5. Warum sprach man von einem Wirtschaftswunder in der BRD und der DDR?
6. Warum war 1970 so wichtig?

Copyright © 1989 by Holt, Rinehart and Winston, Inc. All rights reserved.

KAPITEL 12
ENTSCHEIDUNGEN
PART ONE

I. UND SIE?

Fernsehinterview. A television reporter is interviewing students and young professionals to find out the things that concern them the most. After each person speaks, underline the letter of the item that best completes the statement about each exchange. You will hear each speaker twice.

BEISPIEL   Sie fragten, was ich mir wünsche. Das ist schwer zu sagen . . . Ich weiß aber ganz genau, was ich nicht brauche, um glücklich und zufrieden zu sein. Ich brauche keinen Mercedes, keinen Beruf mit Prestige . . .

The speaker . . .
  a. knows exactly what would make her happy and content.
  b. would be content with a Mercedes and a prestigious profession.
  <u>c.</u> finds it easier to talk about the things she does not need.

1. The speaker . . .
  a. has been unhappy with his studies since the first day of classes.
  b. finds the shortage of student housing aggravating.
  c. is in agreement with the government's position on student housing.
2. The speaker is dissatisfied with her job because . . .
  a. it does not afford enough social contact.
  b. she thinks she should be paid a higher salary.
  c. there is not enough job security.
3. This speaker . . .
  a. would like a scholarship to study English at an American university.
  b. is frustrated because his English skills have declined in the past three years.
  c. is having trouble finding a job as a translator.

Copyright © 1989 by Holt, Rinehart and Winston, Inc. All rights reserved.   **199**

II. BAUSTEIN 12.1: <u>WÜRDE</u> + INFINITIVE

A. . . . und Funktion *(Streß im Studentenheim!)*

Sie möchten eines Tages im Chefsessel sitzen?

Im Stellenmarkt der Berliner Morgenpost steht Ihre Zukunft

B. Im Büro. The following conversations were overheard in an office on a typical workday. Listen to each person speak and decide whether you hear a form of the conditional (**würde** + infinitive) or a future tense (**werden** + infinitive). Put a check mark in the appropriate column.

BEISPIEL Der Chef ist heute besonders unfreundlich.
Das würde ich nicht so laut sagen. Hier kommt er!

	CONDITIONAL	FUTURE
Beispiel	✓	
1.		
2.		
3.		
4.		
5.		
6.		

*C. Am Arbeitsplatz. Theo should be more courteous to his fellow workers. How should he rephrase the following requests?

Copyright © 1989 by Holt, Rinehart and Winston, Inc. All rights reserved.

BEISPIEL   Herr Friedrich, sprechen Sie langsamer!
Würden Sie bitte langsamer sprechen?

1   2   3   4   5   6

III. BAUSTEIN 12.2: <u>HÄTTE</u>/<u>WÄRE</u>

A. . . . und Funktion *(Keine Zeit.)*

B. Im fremden Land.   A group of foreigners working in the Federal Republic were interviewed about their experiences. Each time you hear someone speak, complete the corresponding "if/then" statement so that it is consistent with what the speaker said. Write your answers in the spaces provided, using a subjunctive form of *haben* or *sein*. You will hear each speaker twice.

BEISPIEL   Her Konstantin: Es gefällt uns eigentlich sehr gut in der Bundesrepublik. Wir haben uns aber noch nicht ganz an das deutsche Essen gewöhnt und wir vermissen einen griechischen Markt. Ein deutscher Markt ist in der Nähe, und er ist sehr gut, aber . . .

Familie Konstantin wäre glücklicher, wenn . . .
ein griechischer Markt in der Nähe wäre.

1. Frau Rutkowski würde es besser finden, wenn . . .

   _____

2. Für Herrn Ahbids Frau wäre es besser, wenn . . .

   _____

3. Fräulein Mielek würde einen Sprachkurs machen, wenn . . .

   _____

*C. Kein positives Image.   Roland and Paul are satisfied with the university they attend, but wish that the town were more livable. Tell what they say.

BEISPIEL   Stadt: nicht so unattraktiv
Wenn die Stadt nur nicht so unattraktiv wäre!

Stadt: größere Parks
Wenn die Stadt nur größere Parks hätte!

1   2   3   4   5   6

Copyright © 1989 by Holt, Rinehart and Winston, Inc. All rights reserved.

IV. BAUSTEIN 12.3: RELATIVE PRONOUNS

A. . . . UND FUNKTION *(Auf dem Arbeitsamt.)*

B. Auf dem Arbeitsamt. Participants in an employment seminar are getting acquainted during a coffee break. Listen to what they say and decide the case of the relative pronoun in each sentence. Put a check mark in the appropriate column. Each sentence will be read twice.

BEISPIEL   Ich machte einen Kurs, der sehr schwierig war.

	NOMINATIVE	ACCUSATIVE	DATIVE	GENITIVE
Beispiel	✓			
1.				
2.				
3.				
4.				
5.				
6.				

*C. Was haben sie gesagt?   The following exchanges were overheard in the lobby of a career counselor's office. Use the cues to give the reply to each statement.

BEISPIEL   Ich suche einen Arbeitsplatz, der freundliche Mitarbeiter hat.
(Büro)
Ich suche ein Büro, das freundliche Mitarbeiter hat.

1   2   3   4   5   6

D. Was ist . . . ?   Use the spoken and written cues to answer the questions. Follow the model.

BEISPIEL   Was ist ein Gehalt?
Geld/man bekommen für seine Arbeit
Ein Gehalt ist Geld, das man für seine Arbeit bekommt.

Copyright © 1989 by Holt, Rinehart and Winston, Inc. All rights reserved.

1. Geld/man bekommen fürs Studium
2. alter deutscher Brauch/man feiern vor der Hochzeit
3. Baum/man schmücken zu Weihnachten
4. nicht sehr ernste Krankheit/man bekommen meistens im Winter

V. BAUSTEIN 12.4: INDEFINITE RELATIVE PRONOUNS

A. . . . und Funktion *(Alternativer Lebensstil.)*

B. Geben Sie Rat!   Hedwig Rein is always giving advice. Listen as several people tell her their problems, then complete the sentences in writing to tell what advice she gives. Use the indefinite relative pronouns **wo** or **was.** You will hear each speaker twice.

BEISPIEL   Ich bin im Moment gar nicht glücklich. Ich habe einfach zu viele Verantwortungen. Ich muß Karriere machen und für meine Familie sorgen. Mir machen viele Dinge Spaß, aber ich habe nie Zeit dafür.

Machen Sie sofort etwas, . . .
was Ihnen Spaß macht.

1. Sagen Sie Ihren Kollegen nichts von dem, . . .

   _____

2. Fahren Sie nach Hawaii, . . .

   _____

3. Kaufen Sie etwas, . . .

   _____

4. Glauben Sie nicht alles, . . .

   _____

C. Ein Spruch für alles!   Herr Trödler has a saying for just about everything. Listen as his friends tell him about things that have happened to them or other people and circle the letter of the proverb he would probably quote. You will hear each speaker twice.

Copyright © 1989 by Holt, Rinehart and Winston, Inc. All rights reserved.

1. a. Wer nicht hören will, muß fühlen.
   b. Wer andern eine Grube gräbt, fällt selbst hinein.
   c. Wer nicht wagt, gewinnt nicht.
2. a. Wer zuletzt lacht, lacht am besten.
   b. Wer die Wahl hat, hat die Qual.
   c. Wer sucht, findet.
3. a. Wer zwei Hasen zugleich will jagen, wird keinen davon nach Hause tragen.
   b. Wer viel ändert, bessert wenig.
   c. Wer nicht kann, was er will, muß wollen, was er kann.

VI. SYNTHESE

A. Warum haben Sie diese Uni gewählt? Imagine that you are contributing to a story on international students for your university newspaper. You are interviewing four students who tell why they have chosen to study at a particular institution. Each person will speak only once, so take brief notes in German as they speak. After all speakers have finished, stop the tape and fill out the chart in English to hand in to your editor.

Notizen

Beate Enger: _____

_____

_____

Jürgen Lohscheidt: _____

_____

_____

Ingrid Dörfler: _____

_____

_____

Wieland Reidt: _____

_____

_____

Copyright © 1989 by Holt, Rinehart and Winston, Inc. All rights reserved.

	Beate	Jürgen	Ingrid	Wieland
sports				
few required courses				
scholarships				
low tuition				
good professional preparation				
cultural opportunities				
social organizations				
dorms				
size of student population				
academic reputation				
location				
Other: _____ _____				

B. Jetzt sprechen Sie! Imagine that you are competing for scholarships and big prizes in a Mr. or Ms. Student International contest. You have made it to the finals, and must now speak extemporaneously in response to questions posed by the moderator. Each question will be followed by a 20-second pause for your response. Remember that the judges are looking for substantial answers in German, so say as much as you can in the time allotted. Good luck!

1   2   3   4

Copyright © 1989 by Holt, Rinehart and Winston, Inc. All rights reserved.

PART TWO

I. BAUSTEIN 12.1: <u>WÜRDE</u> + INFINITIVE

A. Im fremden Land. People have different opinions about how they would react to life or cope with its problems, if suddenly they were living in a foreign country. Using the cues provided and following the model, tell what the following people say.

BEISPIEL   ich/Leben in fremd- Land/schwer finden
   Ich würde das Leben im fremden Land schwer finden.

1. Franz und ich/sich amüsieren//und/die neu- Bräuche/gern/kennenlernen

   _____

   _____

2. du/das Leben/in neu- Land/phantastisch finden//nicht wahr?

   _____

   _____

3. ihr/versuchen//Kontakt mit ander- Deutschen/zu haben

   _____

   _____

4. Unser- Kinder/sich nicht gewöhnen an/ein fremd- Land

   _____

   _____

Copyright © 1989 by Holt, Rinehart and Winston, Inc. All rights reserved.

5. ich/schreiben/viel- Briefe/an mein- best- Freunde zu Hause

_____

_____

6. uns/gefallen/nicht/der Kontakt mit fremd- Menschen//und/wir/sofort/
zurückkommen

_____

_____

B. Was sagen Sie?   Imagine yourself in the following situations.
What would you say?

BEISPIEL   Sie lernen in der Bibliothek, da Sie morgen früh eine wichtige
Prüfung machen. Zwei Studenten an Ihrem Tisch diskutieren
sehr laut.
Würdet ihr bitte nicht so laut sprechen? Ich muß lernen.

1. Jemand ruft Sie an, aber Sie können die Person nicht verstehen.

_____

_____

2. Sie treffen eine Person in einer Disko oder an der Uni und möchten sie
besser kennenlernen.

_____

_____

3. Sie sind in einer neuen Stadt und brauchen Information darüber. Sie
stehen neben einer Person auf der Straße.

_____

_____

4. Sie sind in einem fremden Land und sprechen die Sprache nicht sehr
gut. Eine Person spricht sehr schnell mit Ihnen.

_____

_____

Copyright © 1989 by Holt, Rinehart and Winston, Inc. All rights reserved.

5. Sie brauchen Geld und rufen Ihre Eltern an.

_____

_____

II. BAUSTEIN 12.2: <u>HÄTTE</u>/<u>WÄRE</u>

A. Vorlesungen oder Seminare? Jochen is helping two Canadian
students decide whether they should take a lecture course or a seminar
at the **Universität Wien.** Tell what they say by supplying the appropriate form of **hätte** or **wäre.**

1. Jochen: Was _____ ihr lieber: Vorlesungen oder Seminare?

2. Judy: Ich _____ eigentlich beides gern. Obwohl . . . ein

    Seminar . . . Ich weiß nicht, ob mein Deutsch gut genug dafür

    _____ .

3. Jochen: In einem Seminar _____ du die Möglichkeit, dein

    Deutsch zu verbessern.

4. Judy: Ja, und wie! Ich _____ die Möglichkeit, viele Arbeiten zu

    schreiben. Und genau das _____ schwierig für mich.

    Und ich _____ mit einer schlechten Note sehr unzufrie-

    den.

5. Sue: Aber Judy, ein Seminar _____ nicht so unpersönlich,

    und wir _____ mehr Kontakt mit anderen Studenten. Wir

    _____ nicht in überfüllten Hörsälen . . .

6. Jochen: Und ihr könnt euch ja auf das Seminar vorbereiten. Ihr

    _____ dann bereit (ready) zu diskutieren.

Copyright © 1989 by Holt, Rinehart and Winston, Inc. All rights reserved.   **209**

B. Wenn . . . Unhappy with his summer office job in Zürich, Bruce Hunt is preparing a memo that details some of his grievances. Using the verbs **hätte** and **wäre,** combine elements from both columns to create sentences that tell what he writes.

BEISPIEL   Unsere Arbeit interessanter   mehr Verantwortung
**Unsere Arbeit wäre interessanter, wenn wir mehr Verant-
wortung hätten.**

Arbeit leichter	bessere Karrierechancen
weniger Streß bei der Arbeit	weniger Lärm im Büro
glücklicher	mehr Verantwortung
nicht immer Kopfweh	man bessere Computer
Mitarbeiter zufriedener	Chef nicht so aggressiv
gesunder	meinen eigenen Schreibtisch
bequemer	mehr Fenster im Büro
?	ein eigenes Telefon
	einen Sekretär/eine Sekretärin
	einen besseren Kopierer
	mehr WCs
	?

1. _____

   _____

2. _____

   _____

3. _____

   _____

4. _____

   _____

5. _____

   _____

6. _____

   _____

Copyright © 1989 by Holt, Rinehart and Winston, Inc. All rights reserved.

C. Und Sie? Choose from the following items to create "if/then" sentences that would be true for you.

eine eigene Wohnung	Schmerzen
Angst	viel Geld
schlechte Noten	finanzielle Schwierigkeiten
Durst	Urlaub
mehr Zeit	viel Streß
keine Freunde	Hunger
?	?

BEISPIEL **Wenn ich Durst hätte, würde ich in die nächste Gaststätte gehen.**
or:
Ich würde in die nächste Gaststätte gehen, wenn ich Durst hätte.

1. _____

_____

2. _____

_____

3. _____

_____

4. _____

_____

Copyright © 1989 by Holt, Rinehart and Winston, Inc. All rights reserved.

<pre>
in der Schweiz   arm
fit   nervös
selbständig   in der Bundesrepublik
faul   idealistisch
müde   in Österreich
sehr stark   älter
immer allein   intelligent
        ?   ?
</pre>

BEISPIEL **Wenn ich jetzt in der Bundesrepublik wäre, würde ich viel Deutsch sprechen.**
or:
Ich würde viel Deutsch sprechen, wenn ich jetzt in der Bundesrepublik wäre.

5. _____

_____

6. _____

_____

7. _____

_____

8. _____

_____

III. BAUSTEIN 12.3: RELATIVE PRONOUNS

A. Das Leben ist nicht immer leicht.   A group of people are talking about life's problems. Complete their statements by filling in the blank with the appropriate relative pronoun.

1. Der Verkehr in den Städten wird ein immer größeres Problem,

_____ nicht so leicht zu lösen ist.

2. Ja, aber die Leute, _____ am meisten diskutieren, wollen

auch nicht zu Fuß zum Geschäft oder zur Arbeit gehen.

Copyright © 1989 by Holt, Rinehart and Winston, Inc. All rights reserved.   **212**

3. Aber es gibt doch Busse und U-Bahnen, mit _____ man

   genau so schnell wie mit dem eigenen Auto fährt. Das ist eine Lösung, an

   _____ man sich gewöhnen kann.

4. Die Politiker, _____ uns so viel versprachen, tun jetzt auch

   nichts mehr! Sehen sie die Probleme, um _____ wir uns

   Sorgen machen? Nein!

5. Und die Energie, _____ die großen Industrien verschwen-

   den . . .

6. Aber jeder Mensch, _____ in einer modernen Gesellschaft

   lebt, tut das doch auch! Die Waschmaschine, in _____ du

   deine Kleider wäschst, die Dusche, unter _____ du jeden

   Tag stehst, verschwenden auch zuviel. Es sind nicht nur die Industrien,

   _____ man die Verantwortung dafür geben soll.

B. Die Redakteurin.   (Editor). As a newspaper editor, Anneliese
Trapp refers to her notes and combines shorter sentences to form
longer ones. How might she rephrase the following pairs of sentences?
Be sure to use the appropriate relative pronoun in each combination.

BEISPIEL   Der Verkehr wird jedes Jahr schrecklicher. Viele Bürger ärgern
           sich darüber.
           **Der Verkehr, über den sich viele Bürger ärgern, wird jedes
           Jahr schrecklicher.**

1. Die Sanierung des historischen Rathauses macht jetzt viel Fortschritt.
   Der saure Regen zerstörte es.

   _____

   _____

Copyright © 1989 by Holt, Rinehart and Winston, Inc. All rights reserved.

2. Die Wohnungsprobleme sind nicht leicht zu lösen. Man findet sie überall in dieser Gegend.

_____

_____

3. Man gewöhnt sich einfach nicht an den Lärm. Man hört ihn in der ganzen Stadt.

_____

_____

4. Die neuen Studentenheime werden mehr als 40 Mio. Mark kosten. Sie sollen neben der Bibliothek stehen.

_____

_____

5. Viele Geschäfte in der Unigegend sind zu teuer für Studenten. Man machte sie in den letzten zwei Jahren auf.

_____

_____

IV. BAUSTEIN 12.4: INDEFINITE RELATIVE PRONOUNS

A. Kaum zu glauben! The Smiths are reading the evening newspaper after dinner. Translate their comments for a German visitor. Use the indefinite relative pronouns **was** or **wo.**

1. This is the worst winter in ten years, which everyone knows.

_____

2. A family lost everything (that) they had.

_____

Copyright © 1989 by Holt, Rinehart and Winston, Inc. All rights reserved. **214**

3. The department store Horten, where Else's daughter works, is closing.

_____

4. Nothing (that) I read here is interesting.

_____

B. Und was meinen Sie? Complete the following sentences so that they are true for you.

1. _____ , was ich gar

nicht glauben kann.

2. Alles, _____ , ist

_____ .

3. Nichts, _____ , ist

_____ .

4. New York, _____ ,

ist _____ .

V. SYNTHESE

A. Imagine that you are a German student at the university in Marburg. Using this chapter's **Einführung** and the accompanying **Land und Leute** reading as a guide, write a paragraph telling what you have liked and disliked about your educational experience from school age to the university. Use a separate piece of paper.

B. As a journalist, you have just been commissioned by *Rolling Stone* magazine to write an article on the **Alternativen-Szene** in Vienna and Berlin. Research the topic by referring to the **Synthese** and **Land und Leute** sections and write down in German key words or phrases that convey the essence of the Alternative movement. Then use your notes to write a one-paragraph report on a separate piece of paper.

Copyright © 1989 by Holt, Rinehart and Winston, Inc. All rights reserved.

Notizen

Verein in Wien; 146 Gruppen als Mitglieder . . . _____

_____

_____

_____

_____

_____

_____

Copyright © 1989 by Holt, Rinehart and Winston, Inc. All rights reserved.

KAPITEL 13 ÖFFENTLICHE UND PERSÖNLICHE MEINUNG

PART ONE

I. UND SIE?

Was sagen sie? Listen to the speakers discuss each topic, then underline the letter of the expression that best completes the statement about what was said.

BEISPIEL   Which of the following expressions best describes what Herr Martin has said?
a. Du hast recht.   <u>b.</u> Ich bin damit gar nicht einverstanden.   c. Wirklich?

1. a. Es scheint mir, daß Frauen sich nicht für Politik interessieren.
    b. Das stört mich nicht.   c. Es ist doch klar, daß das nicht gut ist.
2. a. Das stimmt doch gar nicht.   b. Ich bin ganz Ihrer Meinung.
    c. Das wollte ich gerade sagen.
3. a. Spinnst du?   b. Prima Idee!   c. Das ist doch ein Vorurteil.
4. a. Ich bin damit einverstanden.   b. Ich bin dagegen.   c. Ich bin ganz anderer Meinung.

II. BAUSTEIN 13.1: SUBJUNCTIVE MOOD; SUBJUNCTIVE OF MODAL VERBS

A. . . . und Funktion *(Der Kandidat.)*

B. Nach dem Wahltag.   (After election day.) The following comments were heard after election day. For each comment, decide

Copyright © 1989 by Holt, Rinehart and Winston, Inc. All rights reserved.   **217**

whether the modal verb is in the indicative or in the subjunctive. Put a check mark in the appropriate column. You will hear each sentence twice.

BEISPIEL   Ich konnte mich einfach nicht entscheiden.

	INDICATIVE	**SUBJUNCTIVE**
Beispiel	✓	
1.	_____	_____
2.	_____	_____
3.	_____	_____
4.	_____	_____
5.	_____	_____
6.	_____	_____

*C. Höflicher, bitte!   Herbert works in the customer services department of a large store. How would he rephrase the following to sound more polite?

BEISPIEL   Kann ich Ihnen helfen?
           Könnte ich Ihnen helfen?

1   2   3   4   5   6

III.   BAUSTEIN 13.2: SUBJUNCTIVE OF REGULAR AND MIXED VERBS

A.   . . . und Funktion (*Nicht nur Frauensache.*)

B. Wie Oma es sieht.   Ulrike and Manfred want to get married and are trying to convince Ulrike's grandmother that they can handle the responsibilities of married life. Listen to their conversation and for each **wenn**-sentence you hear, determine from the context whether the sentence is in the indicative or the subjunctive. Put a check mark in the appropriate column. You will hear each sentence twice.

Copyright © 1989 by Holt, Rinehart and Winston, Inc. All rights reserved.   **218**

BEISPIEL   Manfred und ich haben uns entschieden zu heiraten. Wir wären sehr glücklich, wenn du deine Meinung darüber ändertest.

	INDICATIVE	**SUBJUNCTIVE**
Beispiel	_____	_____✓_____
1.	_____	_____
2.	_____	_____
3.	_____	_____
4.	_____	_____
5.	_____	_____
6.	_____	_____

*C. Öffentliche Meinung.   Individual citizens at a town meeting are expressing their opinions on various topics. The group then responds in agreement, wishing that the conditions described were not the case. Follow the model to tell what they say.

BEISPIEL   Frau Weiner: Der Lärm von der Fabrik stört die Nachbarn.
Wenn der Lärm nur nicht die Nachbarn störte!

1   2   3   4   5   6

*D. Herr Blüm wüßte alles!   The employees of a statistical survey institute are about to conduct a poll, but they express doubts about their new section leader. Use the cues to say that the former section leader, Herr Blüm, would do all the things mentioned.

BEISPIEL   Hoffentlich bringt er einen Kugelschreiber mit.
Herr Blüm brächte einen Kugelschreiber mit.

1   2   3   4   5   6   7   8

Copyright © 1989 by Holt, Rinehart and Winston, Inc. All rights reserved.

IV. BAUSTEIN 13.3: SUBJUNCTIVE OF IRREGULAR VERBS

A. . . . und Funktion *(Nichtraucher haben auch Rechte.)*

B. Fragen Sie Doktor Fried!   Dr. Fried has a call-in radio show on which she gives advice and proposes solutions to people's everyday problems. Listen to what each person says, then complete Dr. Fried's advice in writing. Include the subjunctive form of one of the verbs listed below in each answer. You will hear each problem twice.

BEISPIEL   Ich wohne in einer sehr lauten Nachbarschaft. Der Lärm vom Verkehr ist schrecklich, und die Stereoanlage meines Nachbarn macht mich auch nervös.

Sie wären bestimmt glücklicher, wenn . . .
Sie bald umzögen.

bleiben	sich entscheiden	fahren	kommen
umziehen	treffen	schlafen	sprechen
ausgehen	tun	lesen	ausgeben

1. Ihr Leben wäre weniger hektisch, wenn . . .

   _____

2. Ich fände es besser, wenn . . .

   _____

3. Es wäre besser für Ihre Gesundheit, wenn . . .

   _____

4. Obwohl Sie Sicherheit am Arbeitsplatz haben, fände ich es besser, wenn . . .

   _____

*C. Diskussionen.   Students in a sociology class are role-playing and discussing how they would react to various situations. Tell how each of them responds to the question: **"Was täten Sie, wenn Ihre Frau berufstätig sein wollte?"**

Copyright © 1989 by Holt, Rinehart and Winston, Inc. All rights reserved.

BEISPIEL   Erik: (das) einfach nicht gehen
            Das ginge einfach nicht.

            Jens: dagegen sprechen
                Ich spräche dagegen.

1   2   3   4   5   6

Now use the cues to tell how the following people responded to the question: **"Was täten Sie, wenn Ihr Mann keinen Beruf hätte und Hausmann sein wollte?"**

7   8   9   10   11   12   13

V. BAUSTEIN 13.4: PAST-TIME SUBJUNCTIVE

A. . . . und Funktion *(Umweltschutz beginnt zu Hause.)*

B. Schon wieder Streit!   (Another argument!) When Michael and Berta argue, they often blame each other for things that didn't work out. Listen to some of the things they say and tell whether each clause is in the present or past-time subjunctive. Underline the correct word. You will hear each sentence twice.

BEISPIEL   Wenn du nicht so unhöflich gewesen wärest, wäre meine Mutter
            länger geblieben!

Beispiel   present <u>past</u> / / present <u>past</u>

1. present past / / present past   2. present past / / present past
3. present past / / present past   4. present past / / present past
5. present past / / present past   6. present past / / present past

*C. Wenn ich das gewußt hätte . . . ! When the local authorities remind her to comply with the city's trash collection regulations, Joan explains what she would have done differently if she had only known the rules. Follow the example to tell what she says.

BEISPIEL   das gar nicht machen
            Ich hätte das gar nicht gemacht.

1   2   3   4   5   6

Copyright © 1989 by Holt, Rinehart and Winston, Inc. All rights reserved.

VI. SYNTHESE

A. Meinungen. Listen to the following conversations in which the speakers express opinions about various topics. Circle the letter of the item that best completes the statement about each exchange. You will hear each conversation twice. Now begin.

1. Regarding the strike of the auto workers, the second speaker . . .
   a. is in total agreement with the first speaker's views.
   b. disagrees and expresses disbelief in what the first speaker says.
   c. thinks the strike is inconvenient but agrees with the reasons for it.
2. The second speaker . . .
   a. is in agreement with the first speaker's views that more women are needed in politics but totally disagrees with what the first speaker says about this particular mayor.
   b. is in total agreement with the first speaker that Mrs. Maier's election is a bad choice because she is too radical.
   c. thinks it's nonsense that the first speaker opposes this woman but is willing to be convinced that she's too radical.
3. In regard to smoking, the first speaker . . .
   a. says that nonsmokers have rights too and agrees totally with the second speaker's opinion.
   b. disagrees with the second speaker and maintains that smokers should not have the right to smoke in public.
   c. agrees with the second speaker that nonsmokers have rights, but expresses disbelief in what the second speaker has said about the rights of smokers.

> # Rauchen
> ## verboten

B. Das Universitätsleben. Imagine that a Swiss student is inquiring about life at an American college or university. Write down a few notes in German, then tell the student about some typical aspects of your activities as a student. You may wish to include the following points:

How often you have to write a paper per term;
What types of courses you prefer: lectures or seminars;
How important grades are;

Copyright © 1989 by Holt, Rinehart and Winston, Inc. All rights reserved.

NAME_____ DATE_____ CLASS_____

Whether you live in a dormitory, in an apartment, or at home, and why;
What you do to relax;
What most students on your campus complain about.

Begin when you hear the tone.

Notizen: _____

_____

_____

_____

_____

Copyright © 1989 by Holt, Rinehart and Winston, Inc. All rights reserved.

PART TWO

I. BAUSTEIN 13.1: SUBJUNCTIVE MOOD; SUBJUNCTIVE OF MODAL VERBS

A. So müßte man es machen.   Several people at a public meeting are exchanging their views about what ought to be done to make their town a better place to live in. Using the cues provided and following the model, tell what they say.

BEISPIEL   All- Bürger/müssen/mehr/sich interessieren für/Politik
Alle Bürger müßten sich mehr für die Politik interessieren.

1. Frau/sollen/Bürgermeisterin/dies- Stadt/sein

   _____

2. Wenn/ihr/wollen//so/können/ihr/vieles/ändern

   _____

3. Wenn/wir 16-jährigen/nur/wählen/dürfen

   _____

4. Wenn/Sie/streng- Gesetze/akzeptieren/wollen//dann/können/man/wahr-scheinlich/mehr/tun

   _____

   _____

5. die Stadt/müssen/etwas/dagegen/tun

   _____

Copyright © 1989 by Holt, Rinehart and Winston, Inc. All rights reserved.

6. Wenn die Bürger/mehr/sich engagieren/wollen//sollen/sie/es/d- Politi-
kern/sagen

_____

_____

B. Meiner Meinung nach. Using the modal verbs, write five hypothetical statements in the subjunctive mood that express your personal opinion on any issues of your choice.

BEISPIEL **Meine Stadt könnte viel schöner sein, wenn es weniger
Schnellrestaurants geben würde.**

1. _____

_____

2. _____

_____

3. _____

_____

4. _____

_____

5. _____

_____

Copyright © 1989 by Holt, Rinehart and Winston, Inc. All rights reserved.

II. BAUSTEIN 13.2: SUBJUNCTIVE OF REGULAR AND MIXED VERBS

A. Gleichberechtigung und die Rolle der Frau. A group of friends are voicing their opinions about the role of women. Using the cues provided, complete their statements in the subjunctive mood.

1. Wenn die Frauen mehr Zeit zu Hause _____

   (verbringen), würde es weniger Eheprobleme geben.

2. Du bist aber ein Chauvinist! Wenn die Männer mehr Pflichten

   _____ (teilen), würde es weniger unzufriedene Frauen geben.

3. Wenn die Männer nur _____ (akzeptieren), daß

   Frauen jetzt Karriere machen!

4. Du sprichst, als ob alle Männer so _____ (denken). Das ist

   doch nicht fair! Wenn ich _____ (heiraten), und meine

   Frau berufstätig wäre, wäre ich völlig damit einverstanden.

5. Es _____ (stören) mich nicht, wenn meine Frau das ganze

   Geld _____ (verdienen). Ich _____

   (sorgen) gern für unsere Kinder.

Copyright © 1989 by Holt, Rinehart and Winston, Inc. All rights reserved.

B. Was meinen Sie? Public and personal opinions on current issues can vary considerably. Using the cues provided and following the model, create sentences that reflect your own opinion. For the "then" clause use either **würde** + infinitive or **hätte** or **wäre**.

BEISPIEL   Sonnenenergie entwickeln
Wenn man Sonnenenergie entwickelte, würde man viele Umweltprobleme lösen.

1. mehr Leute sich für _____?_____ engagieren

_____

_____

2. Eltern mehr (weniger) Zeit mit ihren Kindern verbringen

_____

_____

3. Bürger mehr (weniger) über Politik wissen

_____

_____

Copyright © 1989 by Holt, Rinehart and Winston, Inc. All rights reserved.

4. _____?_____ nicht erlauben

_____

_____

5. sich mehr (weniger) Sorgen um _____?_____machen

_____

_____

III. BAUSTEIN 13.3: SUBJUNCTIVE OF IRREGULAR VERBS

A. Die Kandidatin. A speech writer for Ingeborg König has been unable to complete a campaign speech filled with promises. Help him finish the speech by adding the verbs in the subjunctive mood. Some of the verbs given are regular.

Meine Damen und Herren, wenn Sie mich zur Bürgermeisterin

_____ (wählen), _____ (sehen) die Zukunft

anders aus. Zum Beispiel: Für alle Menschen, die Arbeit _____

(suchen), _____ (geben) es einen sicheren Arbeitsplatz. Ihnen

_____ (gefallen) auch Ihre Freizeit mehr, denn jeder

_____ (arbeiten) nur halbtags. Gegen 1 Uhr _____

(verlassen) Sie das Büro oder die Fabrik, _____ (treiben) Sport,

_____ (vergessen) den Streß des täglichen Lebens,

_____ (spielen) mit Ihren Kindern oder _____

(tun), was Ihnen sonst noch Spaß _____ (machen). Und unsere

Stadt _____ (sein) menschenfreundlicher: Ich

_____ (kämpfen) für schöne Parks, große Sportplätze und gute

Copyright © 1989 by Holt, Rinehart and Winston, Inc. All rights reserved.

Schulen. Im Stadtzentrum _____ (fahren) man nicht mit dem

Auto, sondern mit modernen, sauberen Straßenbahnen. Denken Sie daran:

ein neues Leben _____ (beginnen) für Sie!

B. Und Sie?   Imagine that you are running for public office or that you are a speech writer for someone else who is a candidate. Write a campaign speech, either serious or amusing. Be sure to use a number of verbs in the subjunctive to make hypothetical statements or express wishes.

_____

_____

_____

_____

_____

_____

_____

_____

_____

IV. BAUSTEIN 13.4: PAST-TIME SUBJUNCTIVE

A. Um die Amerikaner besser kennenzulernen . . .   While discussing their recent trips to the United States, a group of people say whether or not they or their friends would have done the same thing in order to get to know Americans better. Following the model and using the appropriate form of the past-time subjunctive, recreate their statements.

Copyright © 1989 by Holt, Rinehart and Winston, Inc. All rights reserved.

BEISPIEL   Wir übernachteten immer in einem Luxushotel *(luxury hotel).*
(kein)   Ich hätte in keinem Luxushotel übernachtet.

1. Paul versuchte immer, besonders freundlich zu sein.

   (auch) Ich _____

   _____

2. Wir aßen überall die amerikanischen Spezialitäten.

   (nicht) Hans _____

   _____

3. Wir besuchten viele kleine Dörfer, um die Leute auf dem Land kennenzulernen.

   (auch) Angela _____

   _____

4. Nicole blieb eine Woche allein in New York City.

   (nicht) Ich _____

   _____

5. Friedel und Ulli gingen oft ins Kino.

   (auch) Sepp und Maria, ihr _____

6. Karl amüsierte sich nicht, weil er Angst hatte, Englisch zu sprechen.

   (auch nicht/auch) Annemarie _____

   _____

B. Wenn ich nur . . . Looking back on your own high school and
college experiences so far, there are probably some things that you
wish had been different. Choose from the following items to create
wishes and "if/then" sentences in the past-time subjunctive.

Copyright © 1989 by Holt, Rinehart and Winston, Inc. All rights reserved.   **231**

mehr/weniger Sport treiben
bessere Noten bekommen
nach der Schule halbtags arbeiten
an einem privaten College/an einer
    Staatsuniversität anfangen
mehr/keine Sprachen lernen

den Führerschein früher bekommen
mehr zu Hause im Haushalt helfen
meine Lehrer besser kennenlernen
nicht so faul sein
               ?

BEISPIEL   Wenn ich nur **ein größeres Stipendium bekommen hätte!**

1. Wenn ich nur _____!

2. Wenn ich nur _____!

3. Wenn ____?____ nur _____!

4. Es wäre besser gewesen, wenn _____.

5. Es wäre besser gewesen, wenn _____.

6. Es wäre besser gewesen, wenn _____.

V. SYNTHESE

A. Ein Bericht.   Imagine that you have been asked to prepare a
report for other North American students on people's impressions
about life in the DDR. From the **Synthese** reading in Chapter 13,
write key words and ideas from six comments that represent a broad
range of impressions about the DDR. Then, on a separate sheet of
paper, incorporate the key idea(s) in your report.

Notizen: _____

_____

_____

_____

_____

_____

_____

Copyright © 1989 by Holt, Rinehart and Winston, Inc. All rights reserved.

B. Imagine you are a journalist who is preparing a report for a German magazine on the status of women in your country. Use information from the **Einführung** and **Land und Leute** sections of this chapter to prepare your report. Write your report on a separate piece of paper.

Copyright © 1989 by Holt, Rinehart and Winston, Inc. All rights reserved.

KAPITEL 14 IM SPIEGEL DER PRESSE: WIE UND WO MAN LEBT

PART ONE

I. UND SIE?

A. Wie ist das Wetter in . . . ? Imagine that you prepare international weather maps for Lufthansa, the German airline. You receive weather information on various countries by phone from a central weather station in the Bundesrepublik. Listen to today's report and take brief notes in English. Because of high transatlantic telephone rates you will hear the report only once.

BEISPIEL   Bundesrepublik Deutschland. Im Süden windig und naß, aber im
                Norden sonnig. Leichter Frost im Süden. Tagestemperatur in
                Frankfurt 0 Grad.

Beispiel   Federal Republic of Germany:
                Predicted weather conditions: **In the south windy and wet;
                sunny in the north; light frost in the south**
                Predicted high temperature at destination: **zero degrees in
                Frankfurt**

Copyright © 1989 by Holt, Rinehart and Winston, Inc. All rights reserved.   **235**

1. Holland:

Predicted weather conditions: _____

_____

Predicted high temperature at destination: _____

_____

2. Spain:

Predicted weather conditions: _____

_____

Predicted high temperature at destination: _____

_____

3. Switzerland:

Predicted weather conditions: _____

_____

Predicted high temperature at destination: _____

_____

4. France:

Predicted weather conditions: _____

_____

Predicted high temperature at destination: _____

_____

5. Sweden:

Copyright © 1989 by Holt, Rinehart and Winston, Inc. All rights reserved.

Predicted weather conditions: _____

_____

Predicted high temperature at destination: _____

_____

B. Die Wetterkarte.   Using the symbols and the information you
recorded in activity A, complete the weather map to show the weather
conditions the Lufthansa flight crews will encounter.

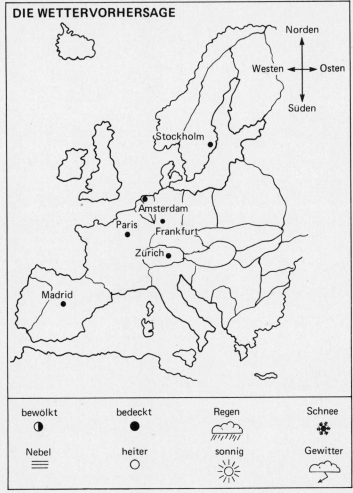

neblig = *cloudy*

Copyright © 1989 by Holt, Rinehart and Winston, Inc. All rights reserved.

II. BAUSTEIN 14.1: PASSIVE VOICE

A. . . . und Funktion *(Kleine Anzeigen)*

B. Freiwilliger Dienst. (Volunteer work.) Benno volunteers regularly to read to the blind. Today he is reading the newspaper to a patient in a community center. Listen as he reads excerpts from the paper and decide whether the active or passive voice is being used. Indicate your answer by putting a check mark in the appropriate column. You will hear each excerpt twice.

BEISPIEL   Ein Einbrecher wird in der Nähe des Stadtparks gesucht.

	ACTIVE	**PASSIVE**
Beispiel	_____	____✓____
1.	_____	_____
2.	_____	_____
3.	_____	_____
4.	_____	_____
5.	_____	_____
6.	_____	_____

C. Aus der Zeitung. Anke asks Udo for more information as he reads advertisements from the newspaper. Listen as Udo reads, then recreate the questions Anke asks.

BEISPIEL   Altmöbel gesucht.
          Von wem?
          Von wem werden Altmöbel gesucht?

1   2   3   4   5   6

Copyright © 1989 by Holt, Rinehart and Winston, Inc. All rights reserved.

III. BAUSTEIN 14.2: PASSIVE-VOICE TENSES: SIMPLE PAST

A. . . . und Funktion *(Unterhaltung)*

B. Das Deutsche Museum.   Rick is taking notes while on a tour of Munich's technical museum. Listen to what the guide says and complete the information by writing the verb according to the example. You will hear each sentence twice.

BEISPIEL   Die erste Autofabrik wurde in dieser Zeit aufgemacht.
            The first automobile factory was opened

1. The first solar energy project _____

2. The first color film _____

3. The first camera _____

4. The first television _____

5. The first cartoon _____

6. The first superhighway _____

*C. Schon letzte Woche!   Karl missed a number of social events while he was out of town on business. Each time he inquires about an event, his assistant tells him that it took place the previous week. Tell what the assistant says.

BEISPIEL   Werden die Theaterkarten heute abgeholt?
            Nein, sie wurden schon letzte Woche abgeholt.

1   2   3   4   5   6

IV. BAUSTEIN 14.3: PASSIVE-VOICE TENSES: PRESENT PERFECT

A. . . . und Funktion *(Kurz berichtet)*

B. Was wird gezeigt?   Sigrid is watching a film review show on Channel 3. Listen to excerpts from the program, and for each passive-voice sentence you hear, indicate the tense of the verb by placing a check mark in the appropriate column. You will hear each excerpt twice.

Copyright © 1989 by Holt, Rinehart and Winston, Inc. All rights reserved.
    239

BEISPIEL Heute diskutieren wir einen russischen Film aus dem Jahre 1928. Dieser Film ist 1984 zum ersten Mal in Europa gezeigt worden.

	PRESENT	SIMPLE PAST	PRESENT PERFECT
Beispiel	_____	_____	✓_____
1.	_____	_____	_____
2.	_____	_____	_____
3.	_____	_____	_____
4.	_____	_____	_____
5.	_____	_____	_____

C. Schlagzeilen. Ingeborg likes to read aloud the newspaper headlines that attract her attention. Following the example, tell how her roomate responds to what Ingeborg reads.

BEISPIEL Sechs Katzen im Autounfall verletzt
Was? Sechs Katzen sind im Autounfall verletzt worden?

1   2   3   4   5   6

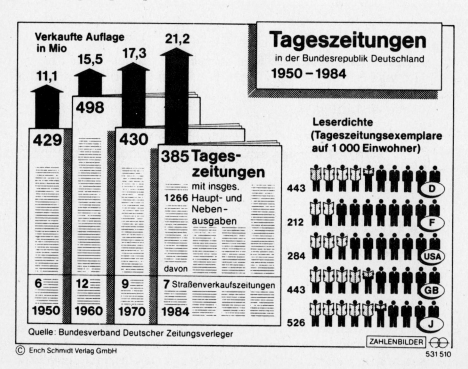

Copyright © 1989 by Holt, Rinehart and Winston, Inc. All rights reserved.

V. BAUSTEIN 14.4: PASSIVE VOICE VS. PARTICIPIAL ADJECTIVES

A. . . . und Funktion (*Küche: Rezept für Heute*)

B. In der Küche mit Küchenchef Heinz. Heinz Huber is a regular guest on a television talk show. Listen to excerpts from some of his cooking demonstrations and decide whether what is being described is a "process" or a "completed action." Put a check mark in the appropriate column. You will hear each excerpt twice.

BEISPIEL   Die Karotten werden zuerst geschält und dann so in 7 cm. dicke Stücke geschnitten.

	PROCESS	COMPLETED ACTION
Beispiel	✓	
1.	_____	_____
2.	_____	_____
3.	_____	_____
4.	_____	_____
5.	_____	_____
6.	_____	_____

*C. Schon gemacht! Udo is an apprentice chef who always gets the job done ahead of time. Tell how he responds to the head chef's inquiries. Follow the model.

BEISPIEL   Wird die Barbecue-Sauce vor Mittag gemacht?
          Die Barbecue-Sauce ist schon gemacht, Herr Renner!

1   2   3   4   5   6

VI. SYNTHESE

A. Ein Reporter berichtet. Listen as Frau Bestohlen talks to a reporter about a burglary that took place in her home. You will then

Copyright © 1989 by Holt, Rinehart and Winston, Inc. All rights reserved.

hear six statements made by the reporter in the article he wrote about the event. Considering what Frau Bestohlen has said, underline **ja** if the statement reflects her account accurately or **nein** if it does not. The passage and the statements will be read twice.

1. Zwischen 6 Uhr 30 und 8 Uhr fünfundvierzig war niemand zu Hause.   ja   nein
2. Als Frau Bestohlen zum Abendessen wieder nach Hause kam, entdeckte sie einen Einbrecher.   ja   nein
3. Der Einbrecher ist durch die Haustür hereingekommen.   ja   nein
4. Eine Stereoanlage, Platten, das Silber, Schmuck, ein Fernseher, zwei Fahrräder und ein Radio wurden gestohlen.   ja   nein
5. Zuerst hatte Frau Bestohlen die Polizei nicht angerufen.   ja   nein
6. Frau Bestohlen weiß, daß die Polizei keinen Erfolg gehabt hat, die Einbrecher zu finden.   ja   nein

B. Möchten Sie mich kennenlernen?   Imagine you are going to submit an audio cassette to a German dating service for yourself or someone you know. Describe yourself or the other person and state your or his/her preferences or requirements for a friend or partner. You may plan your tape in the form of brief notes in German in the space provided. Begin speaking when you hear the tone.

Notizen

_____

_____

_____

_____

_____

Copyright © 1989 by Holt, Rinehart and Winston, Inc. All rights reserved.

Durch eine Anzeige
haben wir uns gefunden

Dieser Weg ist schon lange nicht mehr ungewöhnlich.

Durch Heirats- und Bekanntschaftsanzeigen in der
FRANKFURTER RUNDSCHAU wurden schon unzählige
Ehen und Bekanntschaften in allen Teilen der
Bundesrepublik geknüpft.

SIE sollten es einmal probieren

Frankfurter Rundschau
Anzeigenabteilung
Postfach 100660, 6000 Frankfurt am Main 1

Copyright © 1989 by Holt, Rinehart and Winston, Inc. All rights reserved.

PART TWO

I. BAUSTEIN 14.1: PASSIVE VOICE

Auskunft über die Bundesrepublik. Margot, an employee at the German Information Center, is preparing a brochure for travelers. What would the captions for the following topics look like, if she used the active voice and *man* instead?

BEISPIEL   Am Nachmittag wird Kaffee getrunken.
              Am Nachmittag trinkt man Kaffee.

1.   Im Spätwinter wird in vielen Gegenden Karneval gefeiert.

     _____

2.   Gewöhnlich wird Bier, Wein oder Mineralwasser mit dem Essen bestellt.

     _____

     _____

3.   Aspirin wird in der Apotheke gekauft, und Zahnpasta und Seife in der Drogerie.

     _____

     _____

4.   In vielen Geschäften wird Englisch gesprochen.

     _____

5.   Das Hauptessen *(main meal)* wird am Mittag gegessen.

     _____

Copyright © 1989 by Holt, Rinehart and Winston, Inc. All rights reserved.

II. BAUSTEIN 14.2: PASSIVE-VOICE TENSES: SIMPLE PAST

Bemerkenswert! (Noteworthy!) The chief editor of a tabloid is commenting on some possible filler stories for the next edition. Following the model, write the comments he sends on to the staff. Your sentences should be in the same tense as the original.

BEISPIEL   Die Politiker luden den Bürgermeister nicht zum großen Fest ein.
Merkwürdig! **Der Bürgermeister wurde von den Politikern nicht zum großen Fest eingeladen!**

1. Man erwartete 130.000 Fußball-Fans für das Spiel gegen England.

   Verrückt! _____

   _____

2. Die Polizei entdeckte ein Skelett im Keller eines Berliner Krankenhauses.

   Großartig! _____

   _____

3. Beim großen Straßenfest in Wilmersdorf trank man 6.000 Liter Bier.

   Imponierend! _____

   _____

4. Nach der Sanierung erkannte die Familie das eigene Haus nicht.

   Das gibt's doch gar nicht! _____

   _____

5. Ein Junge nahm das letzte Geld einer alten Hamburgerin.

   Schrecklich! _____

   _____

Copyright © 1989 by Holt, Rinehart and Winston, Inc. All rights reserved.

6. In Bayern wählte man eine Frau zur Ministerpräsidentin.

Höchste Zeit! _____

_____

III. BAUSTEIN 14.3: PASSIVE-VOICE TENSES: PRESENT PERFECT

Nachrichten aus und über Berlin.   Choosing from the following verbs, complete the excerpts describing recent events in Berlin.

BEISPIEL   In unserer Stadt **sind** über tausend Bäume durch Autoemissionen **getötet worden.**

zumachen	schicken	reparieren	beantworten	feiern
besuchen	töten	bringen	lösen	

1. Die Fragen über die Zukunft unserer Stadt _____ noch nicht

_____ _____ .

2. In der Aktion „Brot für die Welt'' _____ dieses Jahr 90.000

Pakete nach Afrika _____ _____ .

3. Nach einem schweren Autobahnunfall _____ 37 Leute ins

Krankenhaus _____ _____ .

4. Der 51. Geburtstag des Bürgermeisters _____ letztes Wochen-

ende im Rathaus _____ _____ .

5. Die alten Brücken über den Spreekanal _____ im Sommer

_____ _____ .

6. Unsere Energieprobleme _____ auch dieses Jahr nicht

_____ _____ .

Copyright © 1989 by Holt, Rinehart and Winston, Inc. All rights reserved.

7. Mehr als 10 kleine Geschäfte _____ in unserer Nachbarschaft

_____ _____ .

8. Das internationale Filmfest _____ von 25.000 Menschen

_____ _____ .

Ob in Indien, Brasilien oder im Sahel: Die ökologische Zeitbombe tickt.
›Brot für die Welt‹ fördert Maßnahmen zur Aufforstung und zur Wiedereinführung bodenschonender, kostengünstiger Landbausysteme.
Postfach 476, 7000 Stuttgart 1

Brot für die Welt

Postgiro Köln 500 500-500

IV. BAUSTEIN 14.4: PASSIVE VOICE VS. PARTICIPIAL ADJECTIVES

In der Redaktion.   (In the editor's office.) Irene is working for a newspaper. Her boss, Frau Haas, is very anxious to get things done, but Irene is always a step ahead of her. Using the model as a guide, tell how Irene responds to Frau Haas's commands.

BEISPIEL   Herr Friedl soll sofort die Schreibmaschine reparieren.
Die Schreibmaschine ist schon repariert.

1. Wir müssen den neuen Computer sofort bestellen.

_____

2. Jemand muß die Pakete von der Post abholen.

_____

3. Wir müssen diese Arbeit heute noch machen.

_____

Copyright © 1989 by Holt, Rinehart and Winston, Inc. All rights reserved.

4. Sie müssen den Artikel sofort schreiben.

_____

5. Fräulein Ernst soll sofort die Rechnungen bezahlen.

_____

V. SYNTHESE

A. In meinem Land . . . The **Land und Leute** text (**Die Schweiz: ein Bild der jungen Generation**) gives a ranked list of opinions concerning the **Ideales Persönlichkeitsprofil** and the **Problembereiche** for young people in Switzerland. Study these lists and then write what you or your friends would say are the two most important and the two least important criteria for young people in your country.

IDEALES PERSÖNLICHKEITS-
PROFIL
Die wichtigsten Kriterien:

PROBLEMBEREICHE
Die wichtigsten Bereiche:

1. _____

1. _____

_____

_____

_____

_____

_____

2. _____

2. _____

_____

_____

_____

_____

Copyright © 1989 by Holt, Rinehart and Winston, Inc. All rights reserved.

Die unwichtigsten:

1. _____

   _____

   _____

   _____

2. _____

   _____

   _____

   _____

Die unwichtigsten:

1. _____

   _____

   _____

   _____

2. _____

   _____

   _____

   _____

B. Ein Porträt aus Europa.   Using a separate sheet of paper, write a brief essay on one of the following topics.

1. Mitteleuropa.   Write a portrait of one of the four German-speaking countries. Focus on history, customs, traditions, or any unique aspect of the place and people that interests you. Draw on cultural detail in the textbook, other sources, or even your own experiences as a tourist in these countries.

2.   Using information in the **Synthese** and **Land und Leute** sections of your textbook, write an essay entitled **Das Bild der Schweiz: Klischee und Wirklichkeit.**

Copyright © 1989 by Holt, Rinehart and Winston, Inc. All rights reserved.   **250**